Praise for *The Unexhausted Leader*

In our performance-driven society, it's no wonder so many Christian leaders are experiencing unprecedented levels of burnout. But is that how the Lord wants us to lead? Lisa Hosler answers with a resounding "No," showing us what it looks like to abide in Christ and allow Him to guide us toward restful productivity.

— **Jim Daly**
President, Focus on the Family

Are you far more exhausted in ministry than you realize? This fast-moving, refreshing new book told by a seasoned leader and engaging storyteller can help you identify weariness in your ministry pace, admit it, and do something about it. Rich in Scripture and practical illustrations, it walks you through the decisions that an effective—but exhausted—Type A leader made not only to find a better pace for herself, but to change the culture of her ministry—and to see God increase its effectiveness because of their new approach.

— **Michael Martin**
President, Evangelical Council for Financial Accountability

For Christian leaders, Lisa's first book is as much a must-read as well-known Covey, Maxwell, and Lencioni works. It's an invitation and a challenge to strengthen your leadership by changing your focus on what matters. Whether you run a local pregnancy help center, pastor a church, or lead a far-reaching ministry, Lisa's story of her own leadership growth will inspire and equip you for yours. Don't pass this book by.

— **Jor-El Godsey**
President, Heartbeat International

D1253236

The Unexhausted Leader will deliver as promised—you will be refreshed, entertained, and infused with hope. But you're in store for so much more than that! The paradigm of the "productive pause" will revolutionize your ministry, your business, your family, your church, your team. The hitch is you're going to have to give up control and let Jesus lead. In exchange, you (and everyone who follows you) gets to enjoy a fruitful ministry without flaming out. Not a bad offer, don't you think?

— **Debra A. Bell**, PhD
Executive Director, Aim Academy

With vivid imagery, candor, and a touch of humor, Lisa unfolds her story of transformation from a weary to a rest-oriented leader. Her straightforward narratives, enriched with numerous examples, usher us toward living in the secret of the "productive pause". Scripturally sound, simply practical, surprisingly strategic for your leadership.

— **Keith E. Yoder**, Ed. D.
Author, Mastering the Art of Presence-Based Leadership

My list of must-read books for leaders is intentionally short. *The Unexhausted Leader* is a new addition to that list. It's an invitation to a counter-cultural approach to life and leadership. If you are willing to wrestle with and integrate its principles, as Lisa has, you will experience your own transformation as a follower of Jesus and an effective, unexhausted leader.

— **Don Riker**
Pastoral Mentor and Ministry/Business Leaders Coach

Every pastor should encourage every leader in their church to read this book. It is a quick and engaging read filled with relevant, practical truths that all of us need to hear and apply to our lives.

— **Beau Eckert**
Senior Pastor, Calvary Church

Jam-packed with biblical and inspiring insights for leaders, Lisa shares practical wisdom about how to seek God with our teams. She says it well, "We can become so focused on our mission, that we have lost sight of the Person behind it." Understanding alignment, agreement, and advancement is worth the price of the whole book.

— **Larry Kreider**
Founder and International Director, DOVE International
Author of more than 40 books

Wisdom, courage, and strength. These words describe Lisa's journey as she took her ministry to a new level. Wisdom in responding to God's nudge to transform her organization. Courage to endure skepticism from herself and others. And strength as she persevered on a sometimes rocky road that led to a revamped, God-glorifying ministry. Readers will be inspired to actively seek God's direction for their organizations.

— **Cynthia C. Hopkins**, MA, Organizational Leadership
Vice President of Center Services & Client Care, Care Net

One trap every leader can fall into is seeing busyness as a status symbol. Lisa tells her own story of leading her organization out of this lifestyle and into a place of restful productivity. This book gives practical suggestions for using a "productive pause" to bring your team to an enjoyable, effective process of decision-making and organizational advancement.

— **Dr. Barry Wissler**
President, HarvestNet International

Known to me as one who genuinely aspires to practice the presence, power, and praise of Christ in the workplace, Lisa has been gifted to live, love, and lead in exemplary ways. This book is a soul-baring look into candid examples of personal trial and Spirit-orchestrated growth. Prepare to be challenged and inspired toward purposeful change!

— **Don Hoover**
Business Steward

In a very personal and professional way, Lisa shares her deep conviction of cooperating with God in His plans and at His pace. With compelling biblical perspective, Lisa calls us to a "productive pause" that all of us as Christian leaders are desperate for as we seek alignment with the Father's heart. A must read for healthy leadership!

— **Kurt Dillinger**
Founder/President, LIFE International

Lisa shares her journey from being a driven, performance-based leader to becoming a rested, kingdom-advancing follower. Woven throughout are examples from Jesus' life and scriptural principles, creating an undeniable urgency for leaders to heed the wisdom of the "productive pause." You and your organization will be transformed beyond imagination as you engage in the principles and practices of this book.

— **Bill Velker**
Senior Vice President of Operations & Prayer Mobilization,
LIFE International

Regardless of the type of ministry you lead, Lisa's book will ring true for you. Her illustrative stories and God-taught lessons demonstrate strategic and yet fully prayerful leadership. The truths of both the "productive pause" and leading your teams to seek and follow God are clearly and powerfully presented.

— **Arthur A. Ellison**
President, 2nd Question

From striving to rest—a reachable goal in life, work, and ministry. Lisa shares her personal journey in a raw and real way and gives scriptural foundations for serving from God's presence. You will be blessed and challenged as you glean the biblical truths and practical steps for embracing a life and ministry of restful productivity.

Jim Price
Senior Pastor, Heritage Fellowship Church

I can wholeheartedly vouch for the paradigm of the "productive pause," having led in this way for the past 17 years after hearing Lisa teach on it. The biblical principles and practical examples in this book make it a must read for anyone leading professionally or in everyday life.

— **Debbie Davenport**
Executive Director, Pregnancy Resources at Cornerstone

"What do you want?" Jesus asked those who looked to Him for ministry. This is also a great question for today. If you are looking for increased personal peace and rest, as well as deeper synergy among your teams, as a fellow practitioner of presence-based leadership and discernment for the past 20 years, I highly recommend this book. It has already become an important resource in my leadership toolbox. Through engaging stories, Lisa unlocks the meaning of the "productive pause" which leads to stronger alignment, agreement, and advancement as you partner with God and others to build His kingdom.

— **Ben Abell**
Executive Pastor, Grace Fellowship Church

THE
Unexhausted
LEADER

LIVING IN THE SECRET OF
THE PRODUCTIVE PAUSE

LISA HOSLER

The names, identifying details, and scenarios regarding some of the people in this book have been changed. Additionally, some of the individuals who were on staff at the time of the writing are no longer staff members.

The Unexhausted Leader
by Lisa Hosler

CONTENTS

Foreword

Weary? Worn thin from constant responsibility? Want to gain increased productivity? Want to see God at work in greater ways? Then pause.

Yes. Pause, that temporary stop in speech or action to regard the situation. Pause before, during, or after labor to gain perspective and to be refreshed.

How? By turning one's attention to the presence of God. Linger there for a time, express your worship, and you will resume your labor with the difference the wisdom of God brings.

God modeled the productive pause in creation. By God's design we bear God's image and learn to work and rest at God's pace for us.

When we pause to intentionally explore deeper relationships within our sphere of influence, we also synergize our fruitfulness. From this grows a fuller capacity in team discernment to advance our mission as an organization.

Yes, there is a productive pause: to reflect, relate, reverence, regard, refresh, renew, replenish, revise, reengage.

In the chapters to follow, Lisa unfolds the story of her inner transformation as a leader and the corresponding transformation of the organization she serves. More than a story, it is also a guide to your own productive pause.

Turn these pages to follow Lisa's articulate, transparent, and straightforward story of her journey. Her example and biblically-anchored practices make for a credible account—as I have observed from its beginning.

— Keith E. Yoder

Prologue

Another late night at the office. At least it was Friday.

Grabbing my keys, I slung my laptop and tote bag over my shoulder. Then I clicked off the lights, stepped outside, and manhandled the front door. The lock was old, so I had to pull on the knob while I shoved myself against the door to turn the key. In the process, my tote bag slid off my arm, and files scattered across the porch.

"Oh great. Just great!" I mumbled as I gathered up the papers.

I grumped to my car, threw everything inside, and tried to switch gears. It had been a full week, and I still had projects to finish up Saturday morning. But then. But then! My husband, Ron, and I were headed to Charlotte, North Carolina, for a special event. Surely, it was the cure I needed for the stress I felt.

Ron promised I would love it. We were going to our first NASCAR race, and he said seeing one live would be way better than watching it on TV. We'd be close enough to feel tiny bits of rubber stinging our faces, and particles of macadam grinding between our teeth. Plus, he cajoled, a little rough-and-tumble entertainment would take my mind off work.

Ron's choice for fun involves speed and noise; mine involves serenity and nature. So the race held no appeal for me except to escape the demands of my job.

He was right about that part. I'd just been through another hectic season at the pregnancy center ministry I led, and I needed a break. Actually, I was beginning to realize there was no such thing as a "hectic season" anymore. Every season was chaotic! They combined into one big pressure cooker, building up steam year after year.

Come to think of it, rubber in my face and grit in my teeth sounded pretty good. It was off to the races for us.

As Ron drove, he kept convincing me I'd enjoy the race. "Here's what you do. Just keep your eye on the 18 car. Watch him try to pass the cars around him. Hopefully, we'll see some good action."

The 18 car was driven by Bobby Labonte. It was owned by a company that made car batteries Ron sold at his hardware store. That made him a loyal Bobby Labonte fan.

"This is gonna be a great race, Lisa! Bobby has a hot engine and he qualified fourteenth. So he has a shot at a win."

Amazingly, the race was riveting. Cars flew by so fast, they became a blur of colors. They passed each other within inches, their engines roaring like a thousand jets. And Bobby did his share of passing—enough to lead thirty-three laps. He was in the top ten for most of the race, and he finished sixth. The four hours whizzed by.

I was hooked. I bought a Bobby Labonte T-shirt on the way out, and Ron said a million "I told you so's." We stopped for ice cream cones and couldn't stop talking about the race. We were two happy larks discovering a shared passion.

But then it happened.

Like it did every Sunday night.

The cloud of busyness began closing in on me. I thought about the week's deadlines, the meetings, the next fundraising event. *Oh shoot—and there's that meeting Tuesday morning. Arrgh! Why did I ever agree to serve on that regional leadership team? As if I'm not busy enough already!*

Ron said, "What's wrong, Lisa?"

"Oh, you know," I sighed. "Just the same old, same old. I'm thinking about everything that's coming up at work."

All the joy from our fun weekend drained right out of me.

We drove to our hotel in silence.

CHAPTER ONE

Owning Up

The gravel crunched and popped under my tires as I wheeled into the parking lot ten minutes late. I raced to the door on my tiptoes to keep the stones from butchering the heels of my shoes.

Another early morning meeting. Another day with too much to do and too little time. As the leader of a mushrooming pregnancy ministry, I was exhausted. Was there no end to meetings? No end to committees? No end to ever-widening ripples of responsibility?

Once inside, I slipped into a small room and joined the executive committee. They were already praying with the guest speakers for our networking meeting. After discussing the flow of the morning, we went into the main area to greet the forty leaders, pastors, and counselors who'd gathered. I shook a few hands as I made my way across the gymnasium à la conference hall for my third dose of caffeine.

The speakers, Keith Yoder and Don Riker, announced their topic as "True Mental Health," explaining that as leaders, we were designed to function with Jesus on the throne of our lives and ministries. Keith said to whatever extent He's not, we're off center, off balance.

Well, something was definitely off in me.

I shifted in my chair, trying to stave off the conviction seeping into my spirit.

My justification went like this: *Please don't tell me there's yet another leadership skill I need to acquire! I'm already depending on God the best way I know how. I'm up at dawn seeking God, and I run as fast and smart as I can all day long. It seems to be working quite well, thank you very much. The ministry is flourishing and growing. Young couples facing unintended pregnancies are coming to the Lord. Babies are being saved. Plus, our effectiveness has garnered national recognition among pregnancy center ministries.*

Still, I knew something was wrong.

When the teaching came to a close, Keith and Don offered to pray for us individually. They placed a few chairs at the front and explained that as God led us to come forward, they would ask the Lord to give them insight and wisdom for us.

Now, these were no ordinary men. They were seasoned servants of God who counseled and mentored senior pastors, ministry leaders, and boards of directors. They were highly regarded and respected by everyone in the room. And they were skilled in discerning the Spirit's wisdom. You'd think that would have made me eager for prayer. But absolutely not.

As much as I knew I needed prayer, I didn't want to receive it in front of five of my staffers who were also at the meeting. What if Keith and Don tuned in to whatever was off-kilter in me? What if they prayed it out loud in front of everyone?

Oh no-ho-ho! There was no way I was going to sit in one of those chairs up front. At least not until every last staffer was prayed for and well on her way to lunch.

That would've been a great plan if my staff had actually *left* after receiving prayer. To my chagrin, they all hung around.

A quick scan of the room revealed two things: I was one of only a few who hadn't gone forward, so if I wanted prayer, my window was closing; and my five ministry comrades were perched on the edge of their seats, looking my way. Oh, brother. There was no getting out of this. I pushed aside my pride and took my place on one of those chairs.

The words I was about to hear would dislodge the cornerstone of my leadership.

You see, for thirteen years I'd led the ministry as a lone ranger. I wasn't a loner per se. I was an encourager by nature and good at identifying and cultivating the various abilities in my staffers. We had great relationships and strong teams. But when it came to vision and strategy, that was my bailiwick and I basically did it solo. I'd hole up with God to figure out what He wanted us to do, discuss it with the board, and sell it to the staff. Because I was affable, a good motivator, and not a dictator, my leadership worked pretty well. It enabled the ministry to hum along without a hitch.

The only hitch seemed to be within me. The weight of it all, the ruthless schedule, the possibilities for expansion that stretched beyond Neptune—call it what you want, it was overwhelming. I was giving my best to the ministry, and it was getting the best of me.

Maybe my words are ringing a few bells for you. Can you relate to being not just hurried but harried? Having not just busy seasons but chronic busyness? Expanding not just your organization but your job description? Filling a leadership role not just in your organization but regionally, even nationally? Feeling not just occasionally fatigued but regularly exhausted? Having a schedule that's not just full but bleeds into your evenings and weekends? After all, isn't that what leaders do? We stop the buck. We work hard and stay late. Our car is last to leave the lot. Our dinners are reheated well after our families have eaten. Not every night, but too many nights.

Keith and Don tapped into an unexpected perspective from the Lord.

"Lisa, we look at the ministry you're serving in, and we wonder, can it get any more successful?" Keith observed. "And there's a sense of excellence and God's favor upon the ministry. And in the midst of that, God is calling you to draw even closer to Him, to spend more time in prayer, seeking and discerning how things are to be done. This will lead to a place of deeper intimacy with God. When you consult with other ministries, this is what you will pass on."

Initially I didn't grasp Keith's point. In my view, we already walked closely with God. We prayed together as a board and staff. And we also provided consultation for other ministries.

Don picked it up from there. "I sense a warning with this, though, Lisa. You as a person and as a ministry—the board, the staff, even some of the volunteers—have been running hard for a long time. A weariness has crept in that will hinder your hearing from God. There needs to be a rest. Not just a week or two off work but a shift into a posture of rest. Entering into His rest. You will find far more effectiveness as you learn this. And it will transform the organization."

I stepped away from the chair not knowing what to think or how to feel. On one hand, the success of the ministry was acknowledged. So that was good. But on the other hand, the weariness cat was out of the bag. On second thought, I knew how I felt. Miffed. Their prayers felt like a rebuke, an exposure of my weakness.

I hurried out of the room, inviting one of my staffers to join me for lunch at a nearby restaurant. We'd barely opened our menus when I blurted out, "Cindy, do I seem weary to you? I mean, I know I've been extra busy, but I think I'm upbeat and ready for any challenge, don't you?"

Cindy was a new staffer and hedged a bit. "Uh, I don't know, Lisa. I guess we're all really busy these days."

Not finding the reassurance I was looking for, I moved on to other topics.

But all afternoon, two words from Keith and Don's prayers honked at me like car horns in a traffic jam. Weary! Rest! Weary! Rest! It felt like a billboard that said "WEARY" was looming over me, threatening to dwarf the persona I'd projected for so long. To me, it was okay to be busy but it wasn't okay to be weary. After all, Scripture exhorted us not to become weary in well-doing.

As much as I wanted to discount the prayer from that morning, I couldn't.

I got home that evening, grabbed my Strong's Concordance from Bible college days, and stood at my desk looking up passages with the word weary in them.

> The people are hungry and weary
> and thirsty in the wilderness.
>
> —2 Samuel 17:29 NKJV

Save me, God,
for the waters have threatened my life.
I have sunk in deep mud,
and there is no foothold;
I have come into deep waters,
and a flood overflows me.
I am weary with my crying;
my throat is parched.

—Psalm 69:1–3 NASB

Thirteen years of fast-paced ministry flashed before me. The busy seasons that became year-round. The annual banquet that grew to three back-to-back banquets to accommodate supporters. Same thing with the Walk for Life fundraiser. The opening of additional locations. The conversion to medical clinics so we could provide ultrasound services. The monthly board meetings, monthly staff meetings, biweekly department meetings. The quarterly newsletter and the appeal letters. The daily everything.

My face was wet with tears. As I read those verses, I was reading about myself. I was slogging through a jungle of excessive busyness. Vines of responsibility were entangling me.

I slumped into my chair and admitted, "I'm weary. Oh my word, I'm weary." As much as I never wanted to grow weary in well-doing, it had happened. I had worn busyness like a badge of honor—thinking of it as the stripes every good leader earned—and walked straight into a bog of weariness.

I sat there for several long minutes, stunned.

Hmph. There was no denying it, no more justifying or defending myself. I had seen myself in the black-and-white, spirit-and-truth words of Scripture—that scalpel that can separate joints from marrow, busyness from weariness. I took a deep breath and owned it: I. Am. Weary.

With my leadership MO falling down around me, I remembered the other word Keith and Don prayed about—rest. Desperate for some insight, I looked up more verses.

"My Presence will go with you, and I will give you rest," God replied when Moses pleaded with Him to lead them into the Promised Land (Ex. 33:14 NIV).

"Truly my soul finds rest in God," said a familiar Psalm (Ps. 62:1 NIV).

Verse after verse linked rest with God's presence.

I get that, I thought. *I've experienced that. In fact, I regularly experience rest when I'm with the Lord each morning. It's the best part of the day. My heart is one with His, my tank is filled, and I roar off to work.*

And I hoped the same was true for my staff, board members, and volunteers. I pictured them too privately seeking the Lord and finding rest and strength in Him.

But Keith and Don's prayer suggested we were to rest at work— "a shift into a posture of rest, entering into His rest," to be exact.

Pardon me, but that is preposterous. Downright irresponsible. Literally impossible. There's work to be done at work. Duh—I think that's why they call it work. No one says, "Bye, Hon, I'm going to rest" and then saunters off to the office to hang out with God all day. Seriously. I think we can all agree that we should seek God on our own time and come to work ready to dig in.

Agitation quickly stole the release I'd felt just moments before, when I admitted to being weary. I simply could not comprehend how resting in the presence of the Lord was appropriate for the work setting.

Sure, we all need to combat weariness with restful, replenishing time with the Lord. But just not at work. Period.

But for what it was worth, that night I owned my exhaustion.

You know, admitting to weariness can be anathema to us leaders. We flaunt our busyness and veil our weariness. But it plagues us all.

Anne Beiler, founder of Auntie Anne's Pretzels, says, "I clearly remember the early years of business when I thought doing things unto the Lord meant perfection. The more I had on my plate, the more pleasing I believed I was to God. It also made me feel important. But it created frustration and a decided lack of enjoyment and rest. I'm grateful that through the years, God taught me, held my hand, and walked with me. I learned to honor Him, seek His guidance, and strive for excellence instead of perfection."

"Weariness and burnout are such threats to pastors and church staff that spiritual and physical health are in one of our five staff commitments," says Beau Eckert, senior pastor of Calvary Church in Lancaster, Pennsylvania. "We state it this way: 'Working hard, resting hard—my family, church, and coworkers need a healthy me.' Burnout doesn't come from just working hard; it comes when we don't also rest hard—with God, with family and friends, with coworkers. Resting isn't just passive inactivity; it's full-on engagement in relaxing, replenishing activity."

A reader poll conducted by Leadership Journal revealed that

nearly 70 percent of respondents were personally familiar with burnout. Here's the breakdown of leaders' answers to the question, Have you experienced burnout in your ministry?

- 18% Yes, I'm fried to a crisp right now.
- 26% Yes, but I'm learning to endure despite the heat.
- 25% Yes, in the past, but I made significant changes and it's gone now.
- 19% I'm not sure if what I had was burnout or something else.
- 12% No, I've never been burned out.

I can relate. I've danced across the hot coals of burnout thinking that if I moved fast enough, it wouldn't harm me.

Maybe you can relate. Maybe you're realizing that the scent of something burning at your church is your own hide. Maybe you're winning the endurance marathon at your ministry but losing the enjoyment. Maybe you're not sure if you're burning out at your business or just fed up with the responsibility, the pressure, the growth, or the nongrowth.

Maybe you've cried out to God, "Is this downward spiral of busyness, exhaustion, and weariness inevitable?" Maybe a good friend has pulled you aside to say, "I don't think God intends for you to live this way."

I know we're not friends yet, but if you'll let me, I'd like to say to you leader to leader, "I don't think God intends for us to live this way." In fact, I know He doesn't.

I know He doesn't, because He's changed the way I live and work. He's taken this type A, overachieving, red-blooded American version of the disciple Peter—I'm a visionary, given to bouts of foot-in-mouth disease, touting faith until the water touches my ankles—and He's essentially said, "I want you to also be like John." John, "the disciple Jesus loved," as John so confidently and correctly called himself. John, who was comfortable enough with Jesus to lean back against Him as they conversed over a meal. John, who learned what it meant to be loved and to relax, even as a Son of Thunder.

Jesus is saying to all of us, "Come to Me, all you who labor and are heavy laden, and I will give you rest. Take My yoke upon you and learn from Me, for I am gentle and lowly in heart, and you will find rest for your souls. For My yoke is easy and My burden is light" (Matt. 11:28–30 NKJV).

Jesus' invitation is the gateway to becoming an unexhausted leader. It's how I moved from weariness to rest. It's what transformed our ministry from busyness to an active awareness of God's presence at work. It's what drew us into corporate intimacy with God and each other. It's what replaced our good ideas with God's far more effective ones. And that's the story of this book: the unexhausted leader and his or her team thrive in the presence of God, on and off the job.

I am no longer dogged by exhaustion. My view of God continues to expand. I'm deeply impacted by authentic relationships with the board and staff. I'm regularly awed by the specific ways God leads the ministry.

Our ministry has been revolutionized. God is worshiped. He is our recognized leader. His higher ways are guiding the direction and widening the scope of our ministry. He's giving us fresh, keen insights into our vision and mission. He's providing powerful strategies to reach people. As the Master Potter, He's shaping and reshaping us. The list goes on.

In this book, I'll tell the story of how God changed our culture and increased our effectiveness through the paradigm of the productive pause. I'll lay out its scriptural foundation, identify its three principles, and share examples of everyday revamping and epic revolution in our ministry. And I'll provide practical tools for implementing it in your own setting.

You may be thinking, *This is a stretch. Rest in God's presence in the work setting? There's a time and a place for everything, and the work environment isn't the time or the place for this. Sunday morning comes to mind!*

I know what you mean. I've been there and thought that. When God first indicated this was the direction He wanted us to go, I was bucking and chafing. It went against every work-driven inclination in my soul. But I was wrong. And I was to find out that true productivity is found in relationship with Him—not solely in my well-intentioned efforts.

Or perhaps you're thinking, *This sounds like the perfect culture for a woman's ministry. But I'm a man, and my teams are comprised primarily of men. We think and work differently from women. We're concrete, ambitious, and outcomes-based. I don't think men are designed for this.*

I hear you. And if it weren't for the men at our ministry and at the churches and businesses that thrive in this paradigm, I may be inclined to agree with you.

Looking beyond the anecdotal evidence, I'm convinced of the biblical precedent for this workplace lifestyle. It's the way Jesus related to the Father and carried out His will. It's the way He operated with His disciples. And it's the way the disciples ministered post-ascension.

As you read this book and begin to function this way with your teams, you will

1. have the joy of giving God the honor He deserves
2. be replenished as your corporate relationship with God flourishes
3. experience deeper relationships and synergy with one another
4. learn to work and rest at God's pace
5. gain increased productivity
6. reap the organizational benefits of team discernment
7. see God at work in your midst in greater ways

There's nothing namby-pamby about this. It doesn't involve sitting around a campfire singing "Kumbaya," and you don't have to be wired like the disciple John. God designed us for mission advancement and intimacy, and He knows how to help us with both, whether we're more like Peter, John, Martha, or Mary.

So whether you're male or female, senior pastor or women's ministry leader, president of your ministry or leader within, CEO of your company or head of a department—if you're inching toward weariness and wondering if it's possible to live as an unexhausted leader, I'm here to say that it is. Engaging with God as a team is the key, and it's absolutely life-changing.

CHAPTER TWO

Undone

In 1985, as a twenty-four-year-old fresh out of a master's program, I was thrilled to be hired as the director of a brand-new pregnancy center ministry in my home state of Pennsylvania. I was an evangelical believer and pro-life, but my primary passion was simply to help people find the Lord. I knew next to nothing about the pro-life movement and absolutely nothing about running a nonprofit.

But I jumped in with starry-eyed enthusiasm and joined the board of directors in the frenzied activities of getting a fledgling ministry to fly.

I was a fledgling as well, and my first attempts at flight were not pretty.

During my first TV interview prior to opening, the reporter asked me about our services. I rattled off my memorized list of pregnancy tests, counseling, and baby clothes, then added, "And we'll also refer the young pregnant women to adoption agencies, job training centers, and uh … Medicare." (Medicare? That's a program for senior citizens!)

Because I'd been doing lots of role plays with the volunteers, when our first client walked in, it seemed like another practice session. I was jolted into reality when she handed me a pickle jar filled with urine for her pregnancy test. We quickly learned to tell clients ahead of time how little urine we needed.

To stay afloat that first year, we held a slew of low-level fundraisers: the bake sale that yielded $300, the $500 spaghetti dinner, and the $1,500 ice cream sandwich cookie sale at the Lebanon County Bologna Fest. We went all out for that one. We built a huge wooden stand and painted a larger-than-life ice cream sandwich cookie on it. We drafted our spouses and formed an assembly line to stuff ice cream into freshly baked chocolate chip cookies. We spent an entire weekend trying to get people to buy our ice cream sandwiches. And we had so many of those concoctions left over that I froze them and fed them to our dog for the next two years.

Despite our first shaky steps, the ministry took off. Lives were impacted. Clients trusted Jesus, babies were carried to term, client couples grew in their communication skills. We developed a post-abortion ministry, an abstinence program for local schools, and sexual abuse counseling.

Six years later, we opened our second location in the hub city of an adjacent county. And five years after that, we acquired a third location from a sister organization.

By 1998, we had steadily grown from one location to three, one paid staffer to fifteen, and thirty volunteers to two hundred. We wanted every woman who faced an unexpected pregnancy to have ready access to a free pregnancy test and support. Adding a fourth location seemed the obvious thing to do. With a little prayer and a lot of grit, we did just that.

The grit consisted of town meetings, fundraising letters, media interviews, and the oh-so-unwise-but-fun use of youth groups to paint client education rooms. At that stage of ministry, we operated on a shredded shoestring budget and didn't hire painters. We fed teenagers instead. Saturday after Saturday, my associate and I took turns showing up at the building armed with OJ and donuts for breakfast, soda and pizza for lunch. We'd open the doors to the starving teens, spike their sugar levels, and then naively place paintbrushes in their hands. They got paint on the floors, faucets, and handrails, and sometimes on the walls.

But it was a blast, it was exhilarating, it was ministry, it was for God, and it was ... well, never-ending.

To be honest, I didn't know any other way to run a ministry. How could I, in good conscience, say no to a need or an opportunity to grow? Wasn't that what we were to do—serve people and grow God's kingdom? Wasn't growth the chief indicator of healthiness?

Growth. Effectiveness. Professionalism. Excellence. Ah yes, I was born for these. Give me a dream, and I'd dream it in 3-D. Point me to a mountain, and I'd scale it barefoot. Tell me about a town that didn't have a pregnancy center, and I'd map out the strategy to be there in a year.

And we were. Over and over again.

But thirteen years into it, there was an element of ministry that had me by the nose. An element that yanked me into the next challenge with mustered-up courage and fading charisma. An element that was relentless.

Case in point: After we opened our fourth location, after we spent two months of Saturdays feeding those teenagers to paint our facility, after our afterburners were burned out, nothing eased up. The pastors' breakfast was a few weeks away. The biggest fundraiser of the year was a few months away. And now instead of overseeing three locations, we were overseeing four.

Arrgh! What was wrong with this impressive picture? This beautiful, kingdom-advancing, life-giving ministry that reached hundreds of women a year and had the favor of believers and churches across our two-county region. What was wrong?

I was about to find out.

The day after that momentous time of prayer with Keith and Don, I drove to work and met with headquarters staffers to pray for our clients. Each morning, as had been our practice for the past five years, we dutifully prayed through a list of anonymous requests, taking turns around the room.

Before we prayed, I asked the staff if any of them were weary.

Every head nodded. My head dropped.

Oh man, I thought. *I lead people in a way that makes them weary. If weariness is contagious, I've contaminated everyone.*

I shared about the prayer I received the day before and ventured that somehow God was going to change things for us.

From there, I headed into a three-hour orientation meeting with my new staffer, Cindy. We made it through our agenda with time to spare, so I said, "We have a whole hour left, and I have a list of seven hefty prayer items. Let's take our time and pray through them conversationally."

Cindy—who was always up for prayer—said, "Sounds good!"

Before I continue, remember that by nature I'm more like Peter than John. I was born with a to-do list in my hand and a megaphone at my mouth. So what you're about to read was as foreign to me then as it may be to you now.

But I hope you won't be put off by it. It's simply the way a sovereign God chose to intervene on behalf of a weary group of His servants.

As I closed my eyes, Keith and Don's prayer from the day before flooded my thoughts. I said, "Father, when people think of our ministry, I don't want their first thought to be about our success or excellence. I want their first thought to be about You. I want You to be on the throne of the ministry so You're the one who's getting glory, not us. And please show us where this weariness is coming from and how in the world we're supposed to rest at work."

I began to picture Jesus on His throne, with the train of His robe filling the temple. To me, His robe symbolized His authority, His righteousness, His supremacy. I prayed, "Jesus, may Your attributes fill every aspect of our ministry."

Cindy began to pray in a way I'd never heard before. She said, "Lord, You are our strong tower, our refuge, our fortress …." The words themselves weren't out of the ordinary. It was the way she said them—with such tenderness and adoration. And it was the sheer quantity of the words. She went on to express many, many of God's titles and characteristics.

Back then, if I were going to praise God in prayer, I would say a few token but heartfelt words like, "Father, You are faithful, You are good. And I have a lot of things I need Your help with." And I'd pray through my list.

But Cindy's list seemed to be praise.

As she went on and on, though, I found myself getting irritated. I thought, *Cindy, if you don't stop praising God soon, we are never going to get to my prayer requests!*

Just then, Cindy began praying about Jesus being on the throne and angels calling out, "Holy, holy, holy."

Hmmm... that's interesting, I thought. *That's what I was picturing—Jesus on the throne. And now Cindy is seeing the same thing.*

Then suddenly, and because God is enthroned on our praises, a tangible sense of God's presence came into the room. It wasn't subtle, serene, or delicate. It was more boulderlike—weighty, daunting, crushing. If I had to define it in one word, I'd use holiness. I'd studied holiness at Bible college, and this wasn't the academic version. This was palpable. Room-filling. It made time stand still.

And it made me feel small. Undone. Sinful.

The room had grown quiet, and I realized it was my turn to pray. I wondered what you should say to the Lord when He seemed so very present. I simply said, "Oh, Lord, You are holy." I couldn't think of anything else to pray.

Cindy continued praying and thanked God for loving us. I thought, *It's a good thing He loves us, or we would be annihilated by His holiness.* I remembered my prayer list, which now seemed like dust compared to the presence of God. Plus, it occurred to me that He was quite capable of taking care of those things without me parroting them to Him. I realized He was far more concerned in that moment with having our complete attention.

I kept my mouth shut so I wouldn't say something lame.

Cindy grew quiet too.

I said to her, "I can't pray anymore. I can't even really talk."

Cindy replied, "Neither can I."

I was struck that she too was at a loss for words.

We remained in silence for some time. Finally, I whispered to Cindy, "I felt like that guy in the Old Testament who said, 'Woe is me! I am a man of unclean lips.'"

Cindy whispered back, "That's exactly what I was thinking!"

I turned to Isaiah 6 and read aloud:

In the year that King Uzziah died I saw the Lord sitting upon a throne, high and lifted up; and the train of his robe filled the temple. Above him stood the seraphim. Each had six wings: with two he covered his face, and with two he covered his feet, and with two he flew. And one called to another and said:

"Holy, holy, holy is the Lord of hosts;
the whole earth is full of his glory!"

And the foundations of the thresholds shook at the voice of him who called, and the house was filled with smoke. And I said: "Woe is me! For I am lost; for I am a man of unclean lips, and I dwell in the midst of a people of unclean lips; for my eyes have seen the King, the Lord of hosts!"

Then one of the seraphim flew to me, having in his hand a burning coal that he had taken with tongs from the altar. And he touched my mouth and said: "Behold, this has touched your lips; your guilt is taken away, and your sin atoned for."

And I heard the voice of the Lord saying, "Whom shall I send, and who will go for us?" Then I said, "Here I am! Send me."

—Isaiah 6:1–8

I glanced at Cindy. She looked as astounded as I felt.

We'd just experienced a shadow of what Isaiah had seen. And like Isaiah, we were undone by the holy presence of the Lord. We were quieted, awed, and somehow refreshed.

I pondered aloud, "This has been really restful. I wonder if that's what Keith and Don were praying about yesterday." Then the left side of my brain kicked in, and I countered, "Of course, you wouldn't want to take a one-time spiritual experience and turn it into an everyday occurrence. In fact, you couldn't."

"I don't know, Lisa," Cindy said. "I think God may be up to something."

It was interesting to me that Cindy, as a new staff member, was playing such a key role in this scenario. She seemed so comfortable with God, but in a reverential way. And she wasn't quick to dismiss what had just happened.

I didn't want to dismiss it either, but as the leader, I wanted to handle it with reason and care. As much as I knew what had happened was very real and very much from God, I didn't know where it would go—if anywhere—from there. And I didn't want to make more out of it than I should.

Yet because of its spiritual weightiness, I decided to share it with the rest of our headquarters staff, without characterizing it as something that might continue. When Cindy and I recounted our prayer time to them, each one could tell something of great significance had taken place.

The next morning, I was out of the office. Looking back on it now, I can see that my absence was providential. It allowed Cindy to lead the prayer time. When the staff gathered to pray for clients, Cindy suggested they start with worship. She'd brought a CD and played a few songs. As the staff quieted their hearts and drew near to God, He drew near to them—and each one experienced His presence in a noteworthy way.

The following day was Friday, and even though Wednesday's prayer time with Cindy had stirred something deep in my spirit, I didn't want to keep it going artificially. So when our staff gathered for prayer, I passed around the client requests as usual. Cindy said, "Lisa, I think we should start with worship."

A strong resistance arose in me. In the way that you can think a paragraph in a split second, I thought, *Listen, Cindy, our supporters aren't paying us to worship; they're paying us to do the work of the ministry. Praying for clients constitutes the work of the ministry. Worship doesn't. Plus, what would the board think? This isn't exactly mission critical. And besides, who do you think you are, suggesting what we should do! I'm in charge here, and I set the spiritual tone for this ministry.*

All that as I heard myself saying, "Okay, maybe for one more day." Despite my inner turmoil, I was eventually able to focus on God, and we had another meaningful time of worship. Cindy played a CD, and we simply sat there reflecting on the truth of the words and the greatness of God.

Afterward, Cindy said, "I don't think we're ever going to be the same."

The realist and skeptic in me replied, "We'll see."

But admittedly, I felt replenished. And remarkably, we got a lot of work done that day. Our minds were more alert, important decisions were made with ease, and projects zipped along. The same was true the following Monday. And the whole next week. And the week after that, as our half hour of prayer for clients turned into an hour of peacefully being with God, each of us taking turns bringing in a favorite worship CD.

It was amazing to me that spending that first hour with God didn't equate to the loss of an hour of productivity. In fact, the opposite happened. Increased time with God led to an exponential increase in productivity. As much as I thought hitting the ground running was the most efficient and effective way for a ministry to function, I was finding that pausing to be with God yielded much greater results. Everyone had a new energy. There was increased joy, greater connection between staffers, a deepened passion for ministry.

The secret of the productive pause was beginning to unfold in our midst.

This concept—which sounds counterintuitive—was proving to be nothing less than divine genius.

Simply put, the productive pause is joining with associates to

1. submit to God's supremacy as the sovereign leader of the organization
2. honor, enjoy, and interact with God and His Word
3. pursue authentic relationships with one another

4. discern the wisdom of God's specific direction

5. apply His superior strategies for mission advancement

These simple practices, which may seem elementary at first glance, are golden. They come from the heart of God, who longs to fellowship with His children, and they cultivate a healthy realignment of our heart and will with His.

God took us on a unique path to get our attention and to institute this new paradigm. Your path will be different. But if you'll walk with Him and in His ways, you and your team will be revitalized by regularly engaging with God. You, too, will never be the same.

CHAPTER THREE

Shifting

My husband, Ron, and I have a small cottage along the Saint Lawrence Seaway, a sparkling clean, freshwater river that connects Lake Ontario in northern New York to the Atlantic Ocean via Canada. During the shipping season, from March through December, we have riverside seats to a procession of watercraft of all shapes, sizes, speeds, and decibel levels—kayaks, skiffs, jet skis, pleasure boats, fishing boats, antique wooden boats, high-speed powerboats, yachts, tour boats, and working freighters.

Most impressive and our personal favorites are the freighters. Some are over 700 feet long—more than two football fields—and 78 feet wide. They come from ports local and international, carrying cargo to and from the Great Lakes. These gentle giants move slowly and rumble quietly. You could be asleep in an Adirondack chair on the dock and not know one just slipped by. But if you're awake and one drifts into view, you'll drop whatever you're doing and gawk at its gargantuan size. It's a veritable city block—five stories high—and temporarily wipes out the scenery on the other side of the river. Our neighbor, who has owned a cottage there for thirty years, told us early on, "You'll never be too busy to stop and watch a freighter go by." And he was right.

41

When we have guests, the first person to spy one creeping past our neighbor's boathouse hollers, "Frrreighter!!!" Instantly, echoes of "Freighter!" are heard inside and outside our cottage. Chaos ensues as sunbathers grab their cameras and scramble to the end of the dock while couch potatoes eject and race to the nearest window. "Frontenac from Canada!" someone shouts as they read the large letters painted on the bow. Or, "That's a Hong Kong flag!" Or, "Hey, the crew is grilling burgers on the upper deck!" Whether it's the first one of the day or the last of a dozen, a freighter moving across the waterscape of our front yard is a showstopper.

Maybe that's why Ron and I set out to learn about these floating beasts—these 15,000-ton welded-steel behemoths that transport nearly double their weight, anything from 28,000 tons of iron ore to a dozen 116-foot wind turbine blades. They travel nineteen miles an hour downriver with the current and seventeen miles an hour upriver. Surprisingly, because of speed limits in the seaway, their wakes are as gentle as they are.

But they don't turn on a dime. They can't. It takes a captain a third of a mile to turn a 500-foot, 8,000-ton ship around. Navigating through the American Narrows, where our cottage is located, takes skill and courage. While the river is wide enough for two freighters to pass, it's not a straight course. It snakes its way between hundreds of islands, making steering challenging and critical. A misjudgment or malfunction could maroon a freighter on a shoal or worse.

A few years ago, a freighter traveled at an awkward angle past our cottage. Before long, warning sirens bellowed to announce lost steering. The hapless vessel collided with a shoal and skidded within a yardstick of a house on a nearby island. Three days and a handful of scuba diver mechanics later, the ship was on its way. The homeowners gained a great story, and the seaway gained a good-humored sign posted near their cottage: "No freighter docking!"

Moral of the story? Ships can't turn quickly. They certainly can't turn without a good steering mechanism. And neither can leaders and organizations.

Tired leaders can't regain their vitality from one good night's sleep, one great worship service, or one dream vacation. Ministries don't become more effective overnight. Churches aren't revived in a day. The culture of a business doesn't improve in a week. And we're all aware of churches, ministries, and businesses that have lost their bearings.

So as you consider the paradigm of the productive pause, know that it takes wisdom to navigate toward new waters, and a bit of time for everyone to get used to them. Like any cultural change in your organization, introducing new ways of seeking God together requires ample communication, consideration of other team members, course corrections when needed, and a heart to follow the Spirit's leading along the way.

When ships turn, their movement is imperceptible unless you lock your gaze on them. The same was true of the transformation at our ministry. It happened over several years and was "slow and steady as she goes."

Slow and steady, yes. But even so—as a captain who'd gotten used to running my own ship—I felt every incremental shift of direction. For me, it was an odd mixture of difficulty and delight.

When we first started to spend time with God, I'd wince at Cindy's face-to-the-wind certainty that a new day was upon us. The very next moment, I'd marvel at the indisputable change God was bringing.

One morning, I was standing near my desk as we gathered to start the day with God. We'd switched from a small meeting room to my office because it had an adjoining area with plenty of space for sitting, standing, or moving about. As I stood there worshiping, looking toward my workspace—the place where I'd sit in my chair and wheel around frantically from my PC to my phone to my projects to my people—all the stress seemed to lift. It was replaced by a peaceful sense of ease. I almost laughed out loud. And in a moment of epiphany, my puny little efforts from my silly little captain's chair shrank to their true size, as if juxtaposed against God's super ability and supreme authority.

Some of the change was a shift in mindset. Other change was visible and tangible.

My concern about whether this was a profitable way for my staff to spend the first hour of the day soon dissipated. Right before my eyes, formerly wilted staffers were invigorated. We began to flourish in the rich, moist soil of God's presence and His Word. We sank our roots into His love. We'd dwell on an aspect of His character during morning worship, voluntarily do a word study on it at night, and share what we learned the next day. Before long, we generated so many Scripture passages and Hebrew and Greek definitions that we each purchased a large three-ring notebook to chronicle our findings. Corporate spiritual vitality led to renewed ministry passion for each of us.

We began to enjoy a new level of camaraderie. We were in this God quest together, and He began to soften the sharp lines of hierarchy within our headquarters staff. Anytime we gathered for worship, there were three to four layers of organizational authority in the room. But the ground isn't pyramid-shaped at the foot of the cross; it's level. And there's a disarming safety in God's presence. Masks came off, hearts opened up, people shared their hurts. Not every morning, but when somebody did, we prayed for them.

One morning, God nudged me to share the disappointment of my infertility. I hesitated because I knew I couldn't do it dry-eyed. After all, as president of the organization, shouldn't I keep a polished exterior and a professional distance? God's prompting was louder than my doubts, so I opened up, tearfully, and received comforting prayer. Afterward, several staffers thanked me for trusting them and for being real. I discovered that in sharing my struggle, I hadn't lost respect but gained it.

Functioning as the body of Christ was no longer nomenclature; it was becoming normative. It migrated into department meetings, where I observed a new level of confidence in staffers and witnessed their freedom to express divergent opinions. Timid staffers grew bolder. Dominant ones became better listeners. As we were more honest and honoring toward one another, meetings became more enjoyable and effective.

Occasionally, I wrestled with thoughts of propriety, professionalism, and the proper place for worship—a church setting. But then I'd think of how worthy God was to be worshiped. And that thought would pin me to the mat every time.

Jesus settled that issue more than two millennia ago, as He spoke with the Samaritan woman at the well.

When He revealed supernatural knowledge about the woman's private life, she saw an opportunity to clear up a nagging question about worship: "Sir, I perceive that you are a prophet. Our fathers worshiped on this mountain, but you say that in Jerusalem is the place where people ought to worship" (John 4:19–20).

Just like Christians today, the Samaritans and the Jews had their own worship preferences. The Samaritans built their temple on Mount Gerizim, and the Jews worshiped in Jerusalem. Which was the right place?

Jesus essentially said, "Neither," but with paradigm-shifting revelation.

He replied, "The hour is coming, and is now here, when the true worshipers will worship the Father in spirit and truth, for the Father is seeking such people to worship him. God is spirit, and those who worship him must worship in spirit and truth" (John 4:23–24).

Now, if Tevye, the Jewish-Russian father in *Fiddler on the Roof,* had been at that well and heard Jesus' response, he would've launched into a rousing chorus of "Tradition"!

We get ourselves in similar huffs over worship. I was certainly in one prior to the shift in our ministry. Mine went like this: You can worship at your church, in your car, in your home, or even outside. Just don't bring it to work, please. If we can all just keep our personal worship off-site, that'll be one less group dynamic we'll have to wrangle through.

But Jesus inaugurated a new concept of worship that had nothing to do with a place, and everything to do with a Person. Jesus had one passion that eclipsed all others as He walked the earth— His Father. And one overarching desire—His Father's glory. His answer to the Samaritan woman indicates that we are welcomed into this same intimate, honoring relationship with our Father.

So contrast Jesus' priorities with our ministry's priorities back in 1998, before God began to transform us. There we were, a group of believers devoted to women and men unprepared for pregnancy. We did lots of good things within the walls of our facilities. We loved on people, led women and men to the Lord, helped them choose life for their babies, and provided the educational and practical resources they needed to parent well.

We were devoted to our clients, but were we devoted to our God? Was God truly on the throne of our ministry? Was He our deepest passion? Was His glory our greatest desire?

If you had asked us back then, we would've said a resounding, "Yes!" And we'd have meant it. I certainly meant it when I said in my newsletter articles or banquet speeches, "We give God all the glory for the lives He's saving and changing."

But if you had poked around in the workaday world of our ministry, you wouldn't have found us engaging with God relationally. I mean in the way that Abraham was a friend of God's. In the way that Moses communed with Him face-to-face. In the way that Jacob wrestled with God, Mary anointed Jesus' feet, Paul answered the Spirit's call to Macedonia, and John felt Christ's love. I mean in that relational, heart-swelling, spirit-and-truth way that Jesus described to the Samaritan woman.

No, if you had poked and prodded, you would've found sincerity, commitment, and dependence on the Lord. You would've observed prayer for clients, gallant efforts on their behalf, heartfelt advocate-to-client relationships. You would've seen brainstorming, five-year strategic planning, number crunching. And every other worthwhile activity that takes place under the fluorescent lights of a typical Christian ministry.

And you would've observed weariness. The telltale sign of long-term busyness absent the corporate, passionate, replenishing pursuit of a Person. A Person who wants to be known, to be close, to be helpful.

Come near to God, and God will come near to you.

—James 4:8 NCV

Those who seek the Lord lack no good thing.

—Psalm 34:10 NIV

The Lord will guide you always;
He will satisfy your needs in a sun-scorched land
and will strengthen your frame.
You will be like a well-watered garden,
like a spring whose waters never fail.

—Isaiah 58:11 NIV

These words yielded the results they promised. As we made it a priority to pursue this amazing Person, this amazing God, He replenished and strengthened us.

We were satisfied. God was being worshiped. We were refreshed in Him and growing closer to one another. All was well.

But God had more. Worship was just the beginning.

Let's peek into an aspect of this paradigm we'll examine more closely later.

We were to discover that having God on the throne of our ministry—knowing Him intimately and worshiping Him corporately—was not only our highest calling and greatest privilege; it was also strategic, because He is strategic.

When God is loved and called upon, He draws near. And He doesn't draw near in a vacuum. He draws near with all of heaven's resources in tow—all of His wisdom, perspective, knowledge, vision, and strategies. He cares about our churches, businesses, and ministries more than we do. And He knows how to operate them better than we do.

He knew, for instance, that a key to reaching an abortion-minded woman was to appeal to the maternal heart He fashioned within her. He also knew that our prior approach—writing slick radio ads to appeal to her career-savvy mindset—would not work. Our approach was sans prayer; His approach was revealed through prayer. And the increase in client calls when we wrote the ads God's way told the story.

God began to strategically revamp our ministry as we spent time with Him, and it's continued to this day. I'll share many more examples as we go along.

But for now, let's focus on this core truth: as much as God cares about our organizations' effectiveness, He cares even more about us as individuals, His sons and daughters. And He draws near to us with oceans of love, mountains of strength, and fountains of living water. This love relationship with our heavenly Father, this emboldening truth that we're His children and not His chattel, forms the foundation of the productive pause.

The productive pause is about a Person, a partnership, and a purpose. The entire context is relational. Our Father is the Person, He's extending to us a family-level partnership, and He wants us to progress with Him in His purpose. He wants to bring transformation to us personally, and to our entire organization.

But transformation happens at the speed of relationship. And relationship takes time.

As we said earlier, ships don't turn on a dime. Shifting into a posture of engaging with God will take time on two levels. It will take periods of time intentionally set aside to be with God. And it will take the passage of time for the shift to have its effect in you, in your team members, and throughout your organization.

When we take that time and alter our course in order to engage God with our teams, He is honored, He replenishes our weary souls, and He directs our gaze toward His God-sized purposes.

This reminds me of a scene from Mark Burnett and Roma Downey's television miniseries *The Bible*. Jesus climbs into Peter's boat and says, "We're going fishing." To which Peter replies, "There are no fish out there at this time of day." With love in His eyes, Jesus says, "Peter, just give me an hour and I will give you a whole new life." Peter retorts, "Who says I want one? I tell you, there are no fish out there!" To prove his point, he casts his net. But Jesus' point is proven instead. Within moments, the net is filled with fish. Glancing sideways at Jesus, Peter can't keep the grin off his face. He casts the net again. This time Jesus helps Peter heave the catch aboard. Stunned, Peter asks, "How did this happen? What did You do?" Jesus says, "I'm giving you the chance to change your life. Peter, come with Me. Give up catching fish, and I will make you a fisher of men." Peter, baffled by this head-spinning experience, asks, "What are we going to do?" Jesus says, "Change the world."

The Peter in us can think that God's ideas are so heavenly minded that they're no earthly good. But God's paradigm of the productive pause is not the stuff of pipe dreams. It's the stuff of His kingdom. It's simple. Straightforward. World-changing. It's how we were designed to function—in close, relational partnership with God and others. It's the opposite of striving alone. It's the antidote to exhaustion.

Jesus is inviting us to come with Him and change the world through our churches, businesses, and ministries as we learn to cultivate a thriving, loving relationship with Him that's both replenishing and productive.

CHAPTER FOUR

The Productive Pause

Take a moment to picture the most stressful season in your annual work cycle. Maybe it's gearing up for the fall ministry launch at your church or the next sermon series. Maybe it's the year-end supporter contacts that hopefully yield a third of your ministry's income. Maybe it's a peak sales season that makes or breaks the year. Whatever it is in your world, bring it front and center in your mind.

Now live there for a few seconds. Smell the acrid pressure. Taste the dreaded deadlines, the daunting decisions, the do or die. Are you feeling it? The strain on your emotions, your thought processes, your physical well-being, your family time, your God time?

When these seasons hit, and especially when they begin to overlap, everything in us cries out for a pause button. We count the months to our next vacation. We're ready for Friday afternoon on Wednesday morning. And Sunday night rolls around far too quickly. But, like all good leaders, we pull ourselves up by our bootstraps and plod into work Monday morning. Or Tuesday morning, for pastors whose weekends ramp up instead of down.

Many of us view hitting the pause button as a final, desperate attempt to salvage our sanity and soothe our souls.

But thankfully, pausing isn't an infrequent reprieve. It isn't relegated to vacations. It is a God-designed, ever-present remedy for our intense lives. A pause button is a bit like the switch on an IV drip that allows a patient to access pain relief. In the workaday world, as I mentioned earlier, I call it the productive pause. When practiced regularly, the productive pause becomes a lifestyle of rejuvenating, intimate, and strategic interaction with God and others.

Interestingly, as much as we frazzled twenty-first-century leaders need the productive pause to assuage our frantic lives, God didn't come up with it just for us. It's a timeless and vital way of life He instituted at the dawn of creation. It's a lifestyle Jesus emulated throughout His earthly mission and then taught to the apostles when they entered ministry, jumping into the fray. And it's a practice they continued after Jesus' ascension.

In this chapter, I'll lay out the scriptural precedent for the productive pause, not just noting its existence but also drilling down into its essence. Embracing these biblical realities enables us to experience God's true intentions. Otherwise, implementing the productive pause as a means to an end will yield disappointing results and, far more important, fall short of the fullness of God's heart for us.

God's Creation Rhythms

Let's start with the creation account, looking for concepts that form the basis for the productive pause: relationship, cooperation, accomplishment, rhythm, enjoyment, rest.

Ah, just reading through that list of words makes me feel lighter already. If you skimmed them, read them again and feel the ease behind the words.

The key players at creation were the Father, the Son, and the Holy Spirit—the Godhead. Throughout Scripture, their relationship with one another is characterized by loving honor and cooperation, shared purpose and passion, distinct roles and responsibilities. Some describe their relationship as a divine dance in which they're facing one another in a beautiful exchange of love and glory. The Father masterminded the earth's blueprint, the Son enacted the plan, the Spirit empowered it. The seismic project they worked on together was completed par excellence, exquisitely choreographed.

I'm most intrigued by the Holy Spirit's disposition at the brink of creation. Genesis 1:2 says He moved over the waters. The Hebrew word for move means "to brood, to be relaxed, to flutter." Just like an adult bird brooding over its nest of eggs, incubating them so they develop and hatch, the Holy Spirit hovered over the waters as the earth was about to be born. My favorite nuance from the Hebrew language is that the Holy Spirit was relaxed. All was well. The plans were laid out. God's will to create the world would unfold seamlessly, everything bursting forth magnificently. The Holy Spirit held this reality in the core of His being and was at peace. Yet He was also filled with excitement, like a pregnant woman glowing with anticipation.

Now, if I were facing a project of such global proportions, I wouldn't be relaxed and at peace. More like stressing, pacing, hyperventilating. I'd be stocking up on tanks of midnight oil and cases of five-hour energy drinks. Wouldn't you?

But Genesis 1 describes a very different scenario. Each day had an ease and a rhythm to it. Read verses 3–31 and you'll feel it, even in the repetitive phrases describing each day of creation: "And there was evening, and there was morning—the first day.... And there was evening, and there was morning—the second day...." Over and over, there was evening, then an implied nighttime, then morning, then daytime—when a particular work of creation took place—and then evening again.

55

God didn't design perpetual daytime and nonstop work for humanity. He lovingly built segments into each twenty-four-hour period so our lives would have a replenishing rhythm. Think about it: fashioned into each of our days is time to work, time to not work, time to sleep, and even time to enjoy.

Enjoyment? In the creation account?

Yes, there was time for God to "enjoy, experience, and gaze upon joyfully." These words comprise the Hebrew word for saw in the phrase "and God saw that it was good" (v. 10). This phrase appears again and again, as God affirms the goodness of His creation. God wasn't a hardhat-wearing, clipboard-toting supervisor making his rounds, observing progress, numbly checking off tasks. "Stars?" Check. "Oceans?" Check. "Mammals?" Check. Quite the opposite. He was personally engaged with His creation and took the time to observe it and enjoy it. I picture Him stooping to pick a handful of ripe, red raspberries, tipping His head to savor the warmth of the noontime sun on His face, and laughing out loud at the ridiculous length of the giraffe's neck.

In the midst of His productive workday, God gazed ... lingered ... savored.

Do we?

Like the Trinity, is our relationship with God and others characterized by loving honor? What level of relaxation do we experience before big projects and during busy seasons? What does our demeanor reveal about where our trust lies? Do our days have a replenishing rhythm of work and rest? Do we take time to enjoy the progress we're making? Are we all business, or do we have mini celebrations with our coworkers?

These are God-instituted behaviors worth adopting, and in the coming chapters I'll share practical ways to do so.

As if enjoyment weren't enough frivolity for God, at the end of the most productive workweek of all time, Scripture says, He rested. Now, when we envision resting, we often think of simply not working. And while that's true, it's only part of the picture. The Hebrew word for rest in Genesis 2:2 does mean "to cease from exertion," but it also means "to celebrate, to be still."

So after six days of creating and enjoying the goodness of His work, God stopped working and started celebrating. The jaw-dropping splendor of creation warranted it. And it was good for His heart. I can imagine the Father whooping it up with the Son and the Spirit, clasping hands and whirling in a circle with Adam and Eve, and afterward sitting quietly to watch the sunset together.

Rest was so good, in fact, God blessed this day of rest and declared it holy. He went on to establish a day each week for rest—the Sabbath. And He offers moment-by-moment rest to His people because He knows it's good for *our* hearts too.

God views rest not as a rare indulgence, or something to be squeezed into a few weeks of vacation, but as a staple of human life. God's rest is not a luxury we can't afford to indulge in; it's a necessity we can't afford to miss out on.

God's version of rest—true rest, as it says in Psalm 62:1—is found in His presence. In other words, the kind of rest that replenishes our souls comes from being with Him, from being still and knowing that He is our Father and we are His children.

And that is why rest is so important to God—it provides the opportunity for relational intimacy. Truly knowing God and being known by Him. Simply being together, content, the way a husband and wife share a meal with few words. The way a dad and son fish side by side, sometimes reveling in their peaceful surroundings and sometimes razzing each other. Or the way two girlfriends hunt for shells on the beach, lost in leisure and the joy of discovery.

I'll say it again. God's rest is not a luxury we can't afford to indulge in; it's a necessity we can't afford to miss out on.

I learned that the hard way a decade or so into full-time ministry, when my penchant for procrastination began taking its toll. Pulling all-nighters had worked in graduate school, where the only thing at stake was my grade on a final exam. But cramming at the ministry during peak busy seasons robbed me and my staff of the joy of working and resting with God.

Take the weeks leading up to our annual banquets. As president, I had to plan the program and share a ministry update. With banquet duties piled on top of everyday responsibilities, I often squeezed speech preparation into the final days before the event. I'd grown accustomed to going full-throttle through the last turn to the checkered flag and assumed everyone else was enjoying the adrenaline rush too.

Problem was, it was stressful for our banquet team, and it was becoming less enjoyable to me as well. Their protests—and the wisdom God was teaching us about His rhythms—finally got my attention.

Little by little, I learned to pace my activities during banquet season and factor in restful time with God. Program preparation started three months out. Plenty of time was built in for prayer to discern God's heart for each banquet. Speech preparation spanned four weeks. As we videotaped client testimonies for the banquet program, we took time to marvel at His miraculous intervention in their lives. Because we consciously journeyed with God through this time, we experienced His restful pace, and the spiritual tone of our banquets deepened. They became moments of true worship and celebration.

A striking evidence of this new rhythm hit me personally one banquet day—a day previously filled with last-minute speech rewrites. Instead, I was strolling on the dirt lane that circles the fields behind our home. It was autumn. Leaves crackled under my feet. Bright orange pumpkins dotted the landscape. A farmer driving a tractor lifted his hat as he passed by. My pace was slowed, my heart was at peace, and I walked and talked with God throughout the afternoon.

Ah ... I was making progress. Walking with God in His rhythms.

The creation account reveals the epitome of relational intimacy within the Godhead, shows us a rejuvenating rhythm throughout the workday, and teaches us a rest that brings a deeper appreciation of God and His handiwork. We were learning to engage in these refreshing realities within our ministry.

Jesus' Lifestyle of Pausing

Let's observe how Jesus' earthly life exemplifies the productive pause, noting words like intimacy, love, strength, comfort, wisdom, oneness, transparency, surrender.

Hmmm.... Which of us couldn't use more of these?

We're familiar with how Jesus withdrew to a desolate place or a mountain to seek the company of His Father. We know that in those hours, vibrant love was exchanged and passionate prayers were spoken—sometimes with loud cries and tears. Through this level of intimacy and interaction with His Father, Jesus received power to begin His public ministry, escaped the crushing crowds to be refueled, and grieved the death of John the Baptist.

Let's look at some additional outcomes of those prayer times.

Luke 6 finds Jesus in an all-night conversation with His Father. The content of these interactions isn't always revealed, but in this particular instance it's readily apparent.

> In these days he went out to the mountain to pray,
> and all night he continued in prayer to God.
> And when day came, he called his disciples and chose
> from them twelve, whom he named apostles.
>
> —Luke 6:12–13

So all night long, Jesus and His Father conferred and agreed upon which twelve men would become apostles—those whom Jesus would send out as His ambassadors.

Now, think with me about this. Jesus had spent weeks, if not months, gathering scores of disciples around Him. He had ample time to observe their strengths and shortcomings. He had everyday interaction with them, and probing conversations. He knew these people.

So you'd think He would have known, all by Himself, whom to entrust with the responsibilities of apostleship.

But Jesus never operated solo. He was in sync with His Father. He did what He saw His Father doing and said what He heard His Father saying. He was one with His Father in heart, will, and actions. And that oneness wasn't instantaneous or simply a Trinity given. It was passionately desired, hard-fought, and intentionally maintained.

Jesus went to His Father with a very specific question: "Who should I choose to become My apostles?" He needed a very specific answer: the names of twelve men. And that's what His night of prayer yielded.

Jesus, Son of God and Son of Man, needed direction, discernment, and wisdom. And He knew where to find it—in the embrace and counsel of His heavenly Father.

What about us?

Are we aware of our need for direction and discernment? As sons and daughters of God, do we seek our heavenly Father for wisdom? To what extent do we desire to be one with Him both relationally and strategically? Does stealing off to "the mountain" to be with God characterize our lives?

These are questions worth pondering as we seek to follow Jesus' example of taking a productive pause with His Father.

Perhaps Jesus' most famous productive pause was the night of His arrest in the Garden of Gethsemane. After holding nothing back—of fact or heart—from the apostles at their last meal together, Jesus led them to a favorite prayer spot. In this treasured place of communion with His Father, a new level of surrender would be forged.

The accounts in the gospels of Matthew and Mark include an important detail. Upon arriving at the garden, Jesus asked some of His disciples to stop and pray while He went farther along with

Peter, James, and John. With the crucifixion closing in on Him, Jesus bared His heart to His three closest partners in ministry, saying, "My soul is very sorrowful, even to death" (Matt. 26:38; Mark 14:34).

Imagine it. Their leader, their teacher, their Lord—the one they turned to for direction and wisdom—was now exceedingly anguished. And He was admitting it to them.

Jesus' transparency flies in the face of traditional decorum, professional distance, and lone ranger leadership. Convinced of His identity as God's Son and secure in His Father's love, Jesus had an internal confidence that permitted personal disclosure. He wanted His disciples to know He was facing the crucifixion as a man, with full-fledged human emotions. Even in the shadow of death, He was modeling. This lesson was about being authentic and letting others know your struggles.

Asking for the disciples' prayer support, Jesus took a few more steps and laid Himself on the anvil of God's will. Against its unyielding surface, He asked His Father if there was any possibility for a Plan B. But there was only Plan A. God's hammer would strike, and Jesus surrendered to it.

That surrender during Jesus' productive pause in the Garden of Gethsemane set the stage for the world's salvation.

Productive pauses are like that. They align our will with God's, enabling His life to flow through our laid-down one—transforming us and touching others.

When was the last time our will was softly bent in the heat of a productive pause with our Father? Is there visible evidence of an alignment of our will with God's—a life flow that's changing us and impacting those around us?

The Disciples Learn to Pause

Jesus lived in the paradigm of the productive pause, and He wanted His disciples to experience it too. On one occasion, He pulled them aside in the midst of active ministry.

Here's how it happened. After He chose and trained the twelve apostles, Jesus sent them out two by two, giving them authority to minister in His name. So that's what they did. They preached repentance, cast out demons, and anointed people for healing.

They returned to Jesus full of tales and testimonies. They were pumped, jazzed, and unwittingly tired. "And he said to them, 'Come away by yourselves to a desolate place and rest a while.' For many were coming and going, and they had no leisure even to eat" (Mark 6:31).

The apostles were operating at breakneck speed, eagerly updating Jesus and skipping meals amid the unending needs.

Now, I'm sure none of us have ever worked straight through a mealtime or eaten at our desk. Or if we have, it's been justified, right?

Well, as justifiable as the disciples' pace may have been, given the rampant needs and opportunities for salvation, Jesus operated at a different pace—the one His Father set forth at creation. The rhythm of work and rest.

The disciples heeded Jesus' wisdom and "went away in the boat to a desolate place by themselves" (Mark 6:32). I picture lively conversations on that boat ride, a hearty meal, and a bit of snoring.

They were together with their Master—debriefing, learning, basking, and resting. The time apart provided much-needed replenishment for their spirits, souls, and bodies.

And it was time well spent, because when they reached the other shore, they were greeted by another large crowd.

But the disciples had learned their lesson. While ministry opportunities are urgent and endless, productive pauses are vital and priceless.

There's nothing that screams urgent and endless like the line items on a budget. Every line represents an essential aspect of ministry or business, and they stack up to a Mount Everest of financial need. Projected income numbers may or may not have enough zeroes when the books are closed. Year after year after year.

Is your heart rate accelerating? Mine is.

What do you do when your trust in God's provision grows lean and conversations in your finance department grow tense?

Here's what we did. We pulled our weary, worried selves aside for a retreat in my home. With the clink of spoons in tomato soup bowls and the comfort of grilled cheese sandwiches, our shoulders relaxed and our laughter returned. We remembered that we liked each other. We worshiped together. And we talked honestly with God and one another about our concerns and our needs. Not just that day, but two more as well. Some situations take more than just a day away.

We persevered to enter into God's rest, and I believe God smiled as He reminded us about the cattle He owns, the ways He provided for us in the past, and the times He pruned the ministry for greater effectiveness. He was honored when we read Old and

New Testament Scriptures recounting the creativity of His provision and the generosity of His people. He was blessed when we listened to each other's ideas and tried to really understand each other's words. And He was proud when we sensed His leading and agreed to step out in faith and trust Him.

In our ministry, that was a necessary and inestimable time with God and one another during a critical season of growth. And by God's grace, we continue to learn the value of the productive pause.

The disciples had learned the lesson in Jesus' presence, but would they remember it in His absence?

They were deeply grieved after Jesus' ascension. But He had promised them "another Helper" (John 14:16) to be with them forever—the Spirit of Truth, who would teach them all things and remind them of everything Jesus had told them (v. 26). So they gave their allegiance to the Holy Spirit as well and learned to seek His direction.

In the book of Acts, the apostles ventured forth in the Holy Spirit's power, boldly proclaiming the gospel and seeing thousands of Jews come to faith. They were right on course, but suddenly the course changed. Through the urging of the Spirit, Peter realized that Gentiles also were to be invited into the family of God. Soon Gentiles were getting saved and Jewish believers were getting riled. A disagreement arose about whether Gentile believers had to be circumcised.

So Peter, Paul, and Barnabas sought counsel from the Holy Spirit. They discerned God's perspective and put it in a letter to be hand-delivered to the Gentile believers.

Here's the account. "We have therefore sent Judas and Silas, who themselves will tell you the same things by word of mouth.

For it has seemed good to the Holy Spirit and to us to lay on you no greater burden than these requirements" (Acts 15:27–28). And it goes on to list the few essential restrictions.

"It has seemed good to the Holy Spirit and to us." The early church leaders spent time in prayer, in discernment, and in discussion, to the point of agreement with God and one another. Because of that consensus gleaned through corporate prayer, they were able to confidently share God's wisdom on the matter.

What about us? Who do we turn to when faced with sticky conflicts and dicey decisions? Do we pull together with key comrades to seek the Spirit of Truth? Have we prayed and discussed issues to the point of being able to say, "It seems good to the Holy Spirit and to us" and then move forward in unity?

Before God taught us about the productive pause, my answers to the questions in this chapter would've been sadly lacking or at best hit or miss. If you're in a similar position, don't dismay. You've picked up this book by design, and God intends to grace you and shape you to connect with Him and others more consistently, more deeply, and more effectively.

As you contemplate the productive pause, remember that its foundation is our relationship with God. God is relational.

I shared earlier about the depth of intimacy and oneness that exists within the Trinity—how they are "toward" one another in life-giving honor. We know from Jesus' prayer in John 17 that God wants us to enter into that oneness as well. Jesus prayed, "[I ask] that they may all be one, just as you, Father, are in me, and I in you, that they also may be in us, so that the world may believe that you have sent me" (John 17:21). This is a multifaceted oneness of heart, mind, purpose, and behavior, but its basis is love.

God is love, and He wants us to receive His love deeply into our hearts, to return that love to Him, to love ourselves, and to release that love to others. If it weren't for others, we could hole up with God in a blissful exchange of love and imagine ourselves already in heaven. But God not only loves us; He loves others as well, reaching out to them with mercy and truth. And He wants us to do the same. He wants us to be "toward" not only Him but also the others in our world.

And therein lies the tension, because we're innately selfish, independent, and ambitious. So God turns up the heat in our lives and draws us into Himself, the all-consuming fire. And in that crucible of intimacy with God, we find our true purpose—to love Him wholeheartedly and to love others as we love ourselves. In that crucible, we find His grace, His wisdom, and His strategic direction for every aspect of our lives. In that crucible, we find surrender as He melds our will with His. In that crucible—the productive pause—we die to ourselves and live in Him.

CHAPTER FIVE

Alignment

The first building that housed our pregnancy center ministry had an alignment problem. The foundation in the back was sinking, which meant the floor in that area slanted into the corner. A closet was there, so you could stack boxes over the rotted floorboards and try to ignore it.

Nearby doorframes weren't square. One was so bad, we had to saw off the top of the door to make it fit the awkward frame. On the second floor, things were a bit worse. And on the third floor, pencils rolled off my desk.

No big deal, right? I just put large erasers on them so they couldn't roll.

But it was a big deal. When a foundation is failing, the alignment of the entire building is compromised, and over time—if nothing is done—a building will collapse.

The foundation of Israel's relationship with God was seriously compromised. So much so, Amos saw God holding a plumb line beside a wall to show just how far Israel had drifted from a right relationship with Him (Amos 7:7–9). Judgment was pending.

Alignment with God was essential to the health of the Jewish nation, and it's essential to the health of our organizations.

That's the first principle of the productive pause:

Honoring lordship brings alignment.

We've talked a lot about being an unexhausted leader. But you know, as appealing as it is to be refreshed and revitalized, it's not the end-all. The end-all is alignment with the inexhaustible leader, Jesus Christ. He is limitless, infinite, beyond searching out, and He Himself is our great reward.

God used those very words to describe Himself to Abraham during a tumultuous time in Abraham's life: "Do not be afraid, Abram. I am your shield, your exceedingly great reward" (Gen. 15:1 NKJV).

Throughout this book, I'll keep reminding us of our supreme goal of knowing Christ and being properly aligned with Him. Paul expresses it in Philippians 3:10–11: "I want to know Christ—yes, to know the power of his resurrection and participation in his sufferings, becoming like him in his death, and so, somehow, attaining to the resurrection from the dead" (NIV).

Paul wanted to be aligned with Christ in relationship and mission. His overarching desire was to be one with Christ, and any benefits he received in addition were simply by-products.

God wants all of us to know Christ more deeply and live in greater oneness with Him and with each other. If this leads to less exhaustion—and it will—that's the icing on the cake. But the goal is Jesus Christ. We can never lose sight of Him.

So why is alignment with Christ so important?

A quick word from Webster, and a couple illustrations from everyday life, will lead us in the right direction.

Alignment is the proper positioning of parts in relation to each other.

So, for example, if the wheels in the front of an automobile are three inches to the left of the wheels in the back, the vehicle isn't properly aligned. Oh, it may move forward—we've all followed one of those cockeyed cars on the highway—but it's not doing it efficiently, and it won't be doing it long-term.

Or take spinal alignment. A primary purpose of our spine is to keep our body in sync with our head. This gives us ultimate functionality. When our spine isn't aligned, things go awry, with problems ranging from simple muscle pain to serious numbness to complete paralysis. Spinal alignment is crucial.

How much more our alignment with Christ! He is the head, we are the body. When a group of people are aligned with Him, they function in unity, maturity, and the fullness of Christ (Eph. 4:11–16). When our teams at work are aligned with Christ, they function in love and productivity, just as He designed.

Which of us wouldn't want that for our teams?

Alignment with Christ isn't a one-time proposition, accomplished when we place our faith in Him and receive His forgiveness and salvation. It's an ongoing process, similar to the periodic adjustments some of us need from chiropractors.

Life happens. We overreact to a staffer's question about a change at our organization, perceiving it as a slam against our leadership. We second-guess an essential renovation at our business when costs run high. We cut off communication at our elders' meeting when we cling to our opinions, holding our fingers in our ears.

Life happens and we get out of alignment. We need an adjustment. We need to be reoriented with our Head.

One of our board members, early on, had the uncanny ability of aligning us with Christ in the midst of intense discussions. When the best minds and brightest visionaries jousted for too long, Kerry softly interjected these words: "Let's pray." He'd lead us in a simple prayer asking God for wisdom, and the atmosphere would change. "Draw near to God, and he will draw near to you" (James 4:8). The Head of the ministry drew near, and His wisdom came with Him. Time and again, Kerry pointed us to Jesus for the adjustments we needed.

Honoring lordship brings alignment.

Breaking It Down

Let's look at a fuller version of this principle and break it down into its three main components.

Because Christ is our Lord and we are His servants, we intentionally honor Him and consciously surrender to His sovereign leadership. This produces alignment.

1. "Because Christ is our Lord and we are His servants ..."

The key players in alignment are Christ and us. So first and foremost, we need to understand who Christ is and who He designed us to be.

As you read the following list of alignment truths, note the extent to which you live them out in your own leadership and life.

- Christ is the Lord. *I am His servant.*
- He's the initiator, the "birther" of the church, business, or organization where I serve. *I'm the responder.*
- He's the owner. *I'm the steward.*
- He's the CEO. *I'm His employee.*
- He's the leader. *I'm the follower.*
- He's the provider. *I'm the receiver.*
- He's the one in control. *I'm the one who obeys.*
- He's the source of every good idea. *I'm the grateful recipient.*
- He's the one who gets the glory. *I'm the one who gives it.*

Christ is on the throne, at the helm, in the driver's seat, calling the shots. And we could go on and on.

In short, Christ is supreme.

Christ's supremacy is an eternal reality, eloquently proclaimed in the book of Colossians:

> He is the image of the invisible God, the firstborn of all creation. For by him all things were created, in heaven and on earth, visible and invisible, whether thrones or dominions or rulers or authorities—all things were created through him and for him. And he is before all things, and in him all things hold together. And he is the head of the body, the church. He is the beginning, the firstborn from the dead, that in everything he might be preeminent.
> —Colossians 1:15–18

"That in everything he might be preeminent." When this is our mindset and heart attitude, it shows up in every aspect of our work lives.

In the early days of our ministry, as I've shared, the needs of our clients and the ministry were preeminent. Because we allowed them to eclipse God, we carried the burden of those needs. And we carried the consequences. Our days were characterized by rushing, busyness, and weariness.

Thankfully, because of God's growing preeminence in our ministry, our days are increasingly characterized by working at God's pace, trusting Him, and experiencing rest.

The Message version of Matthew 11:28–30 describes this transformation:

"Are you tired? Worn out? Burned out ...? Come to me. Get away with me and you'll recover your life. I'll show you how to take a real rest. Walk with me and work with me—watch how I do it. Learn the unforced rhythms of grace. I won't lay anything heavy or ill-fitting on you. Keep company with me and you'll learn to live freely and lightly."

We're learning to walk and work with Jesus. Here's how it looks in any given workweek.

- A weekly staff gathering focused on God through worship, Scripture, interaction, and creatively connecting with Him.

- A short walk to clear our minds and rejuvenate our bodies, individually or with a few others.

- A block of solo time away from the office to get alone with God and glean His perspective.

- A few moments to write up a meaningful verse, to put near our phone or on our bulletin board.

- A portion of time to look into the Word, to engage with God individually and be nourished.

We're learning the unforced rhythms of God's grace.

These rhythms are not just countercultural; they're considered counterproductive in many well-meaning churches, ministries, and Christian businesses. As the leaders of our ministry, we realize we're swimming upstream, but we believe it's of God, and we're teaching our staff members to swim upstream. We've given them permission to replenish in the Lord throughout their workday, providing them with examples like the ones above and encouraging them to touch base with their supervisor if they're led to seek God in other ways.

Because Christ is our Lord and we are His servants, staying closely connected with Him all day long is life-giving, both to the individual and to the organization. As John 15 says, branches that abide in the Vine are healthy and fruitful.

2. "... we intentionally honor Him ..."

Scripture is rife with exhortations to honor and glorify the Lord. So much so, they roll off our tongues like nursery rhymes and roll off our backs like water on a duck.

> Whatever you do, do it all for the glory of God.
> —1 Corinthians 10:31 NIV

> [Speak and serve] with the strength God provides,
> so that in all things God may be praised.
> —1 Peter 4:11 NIV

As much as we believe these Scriptures and want to put them into practice, the crush of busyness and our desire to be responsible, effective leaders often take precedence. So we settle for giving lip service to honoring God and hold on to the vague hope that we're bringing Him glory by the general way we lead and live.

At our ministry, we've learned that it takes intentionality to honor God. It takes focused time. It takes giving God priority in meetings. Even board meetings.

A typical Christian board meeting is much like its secular counterpart, except for an acknowledgement of Christ at the beginning and end. A caricature would look like this: Board members gather around a table to make important decisions for the business, church, or organization, and Jesus is there. He's standing off to the side, waiting to be invited in. Someone opens the meeting in prayer, asks God for wisdom, and Jesus steps closer. For a moment everyone's attention is drawn to the greatness and wisdom of God. Then someone gestures for Jesus to have a seat in the corner, and He humbly complies. Two to three hours later, someone closes in prayer, asking Jesus to bless the decisions they've made. And that's it. The meeting is adjourned.

No one intends for it to be like this, but sadly, we often haven't intended for it to be any other way.

It takes intentionality to honor God.

When God began teaching us to honor Him through worship at the ministry, it first impacted only the staff. But by the end of the second week, after I experienced the depth of transformation within myself and the staff, I became convinced this was no passing phase. This was an outworking of the two gentlemen's prayers about weariness and rest. This was of God. I knew it needed to be ministry-wide and rise to the board level.

Our board was a mix of men and women—a handful of businessmen, a businesswoman, and a homemaker. They were godly, professional, and committed to the work of the ministry. From the beginning, we purposed that the ministry would be founded on prayer. We opened each meeting with a brief time of prayer, and frequently—as I mentioned earlier—prayed midstream over a tough decision, per Kerry's prompting.

Everyone was on board with prayer. But worship? Well, we all know the range of strongly held convictions when it comes to worship—so much so that the phrase worship wars is common Christian vernacular. Our board prayed together and opened the Word together, but we had never honored God through musical worship. (We went on to discover that there are many expressions of honoring God. Musical worship was the method He initially chose to help us align with Him.)

So when I decided to call our chairman, Daryl, to ask if we could worship at board meetings, I didn't know what to expect. I had a good relationship with him and knew he'd at least listen with an open mind.

When Daryl answered the phone, I laid out the whole story for him, from the gentlemen's prayer a few weeks earlier to our time of worship as a staff that morning. To my delight, the first words out of Daryl's mouth were, "That sounds like God. I trust you to keep it in balance." Encouraged by his response, I asked, "Daryl, can we worship at board meetings?" Surprisingly, he said, "Sure. Let's start next month."

Worship at that next board meeting was as bland as unsalted popcorn. I came with three songs from a CD and a copy of the lyrics for everyone. Daryl asked me to share what God had begun within the ministry, and I gave a recap. No one said much, and the looks on their faces ranged from wariness to slight curiosity. I handed out the lyrics and started the CD. It was hard to tell what, if anything, took place during that time of worship. We had our usual time of prayer, and the meeting progressed in typical fashion. In hindsight, along with the music, I should've brought some salty, movie-grade popcorn to liven things up!

No one balked at this new addition to our routine, so worship remained part of our meetings. But with seemingly no impact. In the board's defense, they were exposed to worship in this non-church setting only once a month, while staffers engaged in it daily. It naturally took longer for our board culture to change.

A year after we started worshiping at board meetings, something remarkable happened. When the third song came to an end, there was a hush in the room. Daryl didn't initiate prayer. The silence continued for a minute or so. I looked around, and everyone's countenance was soft, reflective. Daryl asked, "Lisa, do you have any more songs you could play for us?" I replied, "I have the rest of the CD." And Daryl said, "Let's keep worshiping." Forty-five minutes later, when the CD ended, prayers arose from hearts stirred by the grandeur of God. A sense of awe engulfed us. When we finished praying, Daryl commented about how good it was to worship God and how present He seemed to be. Everyone agreed.

We moved into the business section of the meeting and bumped down through the approval of the minutes and a few client services issues. Then we came to finances. God's financial blessing was strong, and we were in a position to retire the mortgages on two of our facilities and become debt free. With a unanimous vote, we agreed to pay off the debts, and then we eagerly focused all our brainpower on the weighty matter of a mortgage-burning ceremony. The men suggested wonderfully wild ways to go about it—anything from a blowtorch to a gas grill to an explosive concoction someone remembered from high school chemistry. The women suggested more dignified, safe options, like handheld lighters or a vanilla-scented candle, with a petite fire extinguisher just in case.

And then Daryl made an observation I'll remember for the rest of my life: "You know, friends, as exciting as it is to pay off these buildings, it pales in comparison to the presence of God we experienced earlier." Heads nodded. "You're right, Daryl," echoed around the room. Tears filled my eyes.

God did it. He arranged for the entire board—together as a group—to encounter His unmistakable presence. And just as the staff had experienced, the board members were profoundly impacted by the Lord's presence.

But it followed an intentional honoring of the Lord, meeting by meeting—even with no clear evidence that anything was changing.

The Lord is worthy of our honor. Period. The impact on Him is immeasurable, regardless of the impact on us. He is the preeminent one, and He deserves and delights in receiving our honor.

3. *"… we consciously surrender to His sovereign leadership"*

This final component of the alignment principle loops back to the first truth about Christ's lordship and invites us to put our behavior where our belief is. This is harder than it sounds. For instance:

- We believe Christ is Lord of our congregation, but how do we react when, after months of corporate prayer, 90 percent of the elders want to move in a direction we disagree with?

- We believe Christ is Lord of our business, but what do we do when the cutthroat business world tempts us to close a deal in a way we wouldn't be proud to explain to our children?

- We believe Christ is Lord of our organization, but do we obey when He wants us to trim back our ministry for greater effectiveness in targeted areas?

Let's do what Jesus did in Gethsemane. Let's cry out to the Father. Let's ask close associates to pray. Let's surrender to God. Let's obey Him. Even to the point of death of self, death of our own great ideas, and death of our work worlds as we've known them.

When God tuned us in to mission drift within our ministry, we were perplexed. We believed we had faithfully followed Him in every expansion of services. We started by serving women unprepared for pregnancy, soon began helping women who'd had an abortion, and before long were providing abstinence education in public schools.

But in all three areas, we kept bumping into women who'd experienced some level of sexual abuse. As God would have it, one of our staffers was schooled in sexual abuse ministry. We prayed, found there were no other Christian ministries providing this type of counseling, and felt led to offer it to our clients. Gradually, groups of women gathered with our staff member for healing— many of them our own volunteers. Over time, a dozen volunteers were well equipped to provide lay counseling for sexually abused women. And many more dozens of clients experienced freedom from the bondage of sexual abuse.

As years went by and sexual abuse ministry enlarged within the scope of our activity, two realities became apparent: (1) ministering to sexually abused women wasn't central to our mission, which focused on the sacredness of preborn human life, and (2) several Christian ministries dealing with sexual abuse had sprung up in our region.

To glean God's direction, we entered into several times of focused prayer. As we prayed, God made it clear we should streamline our services to three main areas—sexual integrity education, crisis pregnancy intervention, and post-abortion restoration. Doing so would enable us to funnel our resources into these primary services for greater impact.

Doing so also meant saying goodbye to a treasured, valuable, long-term staffer and friend. Our sexual abuse ministry had become her main focus, and discontinuing it meant bringing our ministry relationship with her to a close.

Ouch. Pruning hurts. But we surrendered to God's wisdom. And our alignment with Him led to a greater alignment with the core mission He'd given us.

Honoring lordship brings alignment in our work worlds. And for alignment to have integrity, we need it in our personal worlds as well.

I faced a personal alignment issue in my mid twenties—whether I would surrender to God my desire to bear children.

On the day He won, I was driving from one specialist to another with an infertility diagnosis hanging in the air. I gripped the steering wheel with one hand and an ultrasound report with the other. Straining to see the road through tears, I glanced at the doctor's words scrawled at the bottom of the page: "Conception for Lisa will be highly unlikely."

All of a sudden, I found myself repeating a phrase in an abortion-recovery video from our ministry. In the video, a woman coming to terms with her multiple abortions said, "My life, my life. What's happening to my life?"

I'd echoed her words dozens of times as I climbed the rungs from a family doctor to an OB-GYN to an infertility specialist.

Baffled, I asked the Lord, "Why do I keep saying, 'My life, my life. What's happening to my life?'"

The gist of His response was, "Because you think it's your life. But it's not. You've been bought with the precious blood of Jesus Christ. You belong to Me. Lay down your 'right' to have children. Lay down your life."

And so I did. At the intersection of the Fruitville Pike and Route 30, an alignment issue between me and God was settled.

Proper alignment with God is critical to life direction, and it's critical to mission direction.

> Unless a grain of wheat falls into the earth and dies, it remains alone; but if it dies, it bears much fruit....
> If anyone serves me, he must follow me; and where I am, there will my servant be also. If anyone serves me,
> the Father will honor him.
>
> —John 12:24, 26

An invitation to die. An invitation to follow God, serve Him, bear much fruit. An invitation to honor the Lord and experience alignment with Him.

He's worth it.

CHAPTER SIX

A Culture of Honor

The heart of alignment is honor. If you want your church, business, or ministry to be properly aligned with Jesus Christ, you'll want to actively honor Him. Honoring God will set you on course to establish the productive pause within your organization.

So what exactly is honor? And what does it look like in a work setting?

To begin answering these questions, let me take you on a boat ride as my husband and I plied the waters of the Saint Lawrence Seaway, exploring the Thousand Islands.

"Oh my word, Ron! Did you see that duck?" I shouted from the top deck of Uncle Sam's Tour Boat. I'd just spotted a large black duck with an unusually thick neck, a prominent white chest, and a dazzling pattern of light flecks on its dark wings. It was nothing like the ones I was used to seeing in ponds on the farms of Lancaster County. I leaned over the railing to point, and just like that, it vanished.

"I don't see anything," Ron said. "And besides, a duck's a duck. You've seen one, you've seen 'em all." (His response was a lot like mine when he points out an antique boat on the river that looks for all the world like the last one he showed me.)

But there was something special about this disappearing duck.

A few weeks later, while Ron and I were canoeing on a calm stretch of the river, I heard a hauntingly beautiful sound.

"Did you hear that?" I whispered.

"Yeah…," came Ron's unenthusiastic response.

"Some creature is making it! Let's find out what it is."

Just so you get the picture here, the reason we were even in the canoe was for my sake. Ron's version of a good time on the river involves a lot more horsepower and noise. This snail-paced, quiet nature cruise was putting him to sleep.

Nevertheless, he obliged me and paddled toward the sound. It seemed to emanate from a sheltered cove.

Sure enough, a pair of those big black ducks came into view. They were barely visible on the sparkling river; their white speckles provided the perfect camouflage. As we drifted closer, I noticed their crimson eyes. With their regal necks and diamond-studded wings, these were the most magnificent ducks I had ever seen.

Suddenly, one began making a rapid, high-pitched sound, and they dove out of sight.

"What in the world?" I exclaimed. "Ducks can't swim underwater!"

Ron was a bit amazed himself. And when the ducks didn't resurface, he was up for a game of hide-and-seek.

We craned our necks in every direction. Surely, they couldn't stay under much longer.

But they did. Two minutes passed before they came back up, and when they emerged, they were a good distance from us.

By then we knew they spooked easily, so we went into our best stealth-canoe mode and glided toward them.

Not to be outwitted, they let us get within twenty yards and— splash! Gone.

We decided not to disturb them again and rowed back to our cottage. But we were hooked, our curiosity piqued.

A few conversations with locals told the story. The ducks were loons. Common loons, to be precise. They migrate from the south each spring to lakes and rivers in the northern United States and Canada. In the Thousand Islands, they prefer the backwaters that freighters can't navigate and powerboats don't frequent.

Before long, we noticed we weren't the only ones enamored with these stunning waterfowl. Gift shops in the region were filled with loon memorabilia—artwork, wood carvings, key chains, refrigerator magnets, and books. I bought one of the books, and my fascination grew.

I discovered that loons are nearly three feet long, with a wingspan of sixty inches. They can swim underwater for up to three minutes, because their bones are marrow-filled instead of hollow like those of most birds. It's how they elude Curious Georges like me and Ron, and it's how they catch fish. Their agility underwater has earned them the nickname "feathered fish." They have four distinct calls, each with its own meaning. They transport their chicks on their backs to protect them from underwater predators.

The more I learned, the more captivated I became. And Ron wasn't far behind.

Now we're never on the river without searching for loons. Often, Ron spies them before I do. Even our friends have become fans of these feathered fish. A sighting is rare, and when one occurs, there is picture taking and celebrating. Resin loons grace each room of our cottage.

And we've never grown tired of loons. Their striking beauty, unique behavior, and mysterious calls are so compelling. We've yet to see an adult toting chicks, but one day we will.

Appeal. Fascination. Pursuit.

On some level, Ron and I have honor in our hearts toward loons. We value them, we search for them, we enjoy being around them.

How much more appeal does Christ have! How much more fascinating He is! How much more worth pursuing!

He's eternally worthy of honor!

1 Timothy 1:17 declares, "To the King of the ages, immortal, invisible, the only God, be honor and glory forever and ever. Amen."

And we're invited to honor Him all day long.

Psalm 71:8 (KJV) exhorts, "Let my mouth be filled with thy praise and with thy honor all the day."

Hebrew and Greek definitions of honor include phrases like:

- to make weighty
- to magnify
- to glorify
- to prize
- to value
- to revere

Relive your most recent workday for a few seconds. What got your attention? What was magnified in your eyes? To what did you assign the most weight?

Chances are, it was the strategic plan, the struggling staffer, or the budget shortfall.

There's nothing wrong with any of these, and we must focus on them. But when we focus on them exclusively, we lose sight of God.

Our focus becomes our fascination.

Let's look at a couple Scripture passages that show two different ways of going about our business. The first describes us. The second describes Jesus.

Psalm 127:1–2 says, "Unless the Lord builds the house, those who build it labor in vain.... It is in vain that you rise up early and go late to rest, eating the bread of anxious toil; for he gives to his beloved sleep."

So basically, this is the picture of someone—like you and me—who is fixated on and fascinated with work, and consequently "eats the bread of anxious toil" and "labors in vain."

Can you relate? I think the part that stings the most is that our labor is ineffective and futile.

But wait, there's another verse. There's another way to work—Jesus' way. Listen to this.

Jesus had just revealed Himself as Messiah to the Samaritan woman. She rushed to tell everyone that she'd found the Messiah, and the whole village was turning out. The disciples urged Jesus to eat before the mob arrived. And He replied, "My food is to do the will of him who sent me and to accomplish his work" (John 4:34).

Jesus' food—His sustenance, His nourishment—came from being one with His Father. His heart was to love, honor, and obey the Father.

And Jesus' work was far from fruitless, like ours is when we do it solo. On the cross, Jesus was able to say, "It is finished," having accomplished the overarching work of salvation His Father had called Him to.

Doing Things Jesus' Way

How do we follow Jesus' example so we view our work like He did and have it rise from a heart of honoring God?

Here are six ways to partner with the Lord in "building your house"—your church, business, or ministry—by honoring Him in the workplace.

1. Personally honor Christ.

Your ability to lead your organization in honoring Christ is correlated to how much you honor Him privately. Cultivate a posture of honor in your own life. Remember the meaning of honor—to make weighty, magnify, glorify, prize, value, revere. Ask God to show you fresh, deeper ways to honor Him in this season of your life.

We're all familiar with the saying "As goes the captain, so goes the ship." What are you known for, and how is it fleshed out within your business, church, or ministry? At the end of the day, at the end of our lives, we'll want to say, "I grew in knowing Christ."

As an overachiever, I used to pray, "God, please help me accomplish the maximum of what You've designed for me in my lifetime." As lofty as that may sound, there's some self stuff in there—

stuff that's about me and all I did for God. My prayer has changed in the past decade or so. I now pray, "Lord, I want to know You to the fullest extent You've designed for me." That truly is my deepest desire, and anything Christ accomplishes through my life will be for His glory. My glory is in knowing Him.

> I want to know Christ.
> —Philippians 3:10 NIV

2. Invite others to honor Christ with you.

As you're developing a culture of honor, explain to your co-workers in down-to-earth terms why you want to implement new ways of exalting God. Be honest with them about the revelation God is bringing to your own heart. Invite them to join you; don't mandate participation. Start slowly, with less-threatening activities like Bible reading or prayer. Give people time to warm up to the concept and feel comfortable engaging.

You'll recall that I initially chafed at "wasting work time" on God. It took me several weeks to realize its importance and to experience God in meaningful, productive ways. It took our board a full year. Nowadays, brand-new staffers most often readily embrace the culture and soon become grateful for the opportunity to honor God during work.

> Oh, magnify the Lord with me,
> and let us exalt his name together!
> —Psalm 34:3

3. Read the Word together.

Reading God's Word with your associates at work, whether a single verse or a whole chapter, is a powerful way for everyone to align with Him in spirit and in truth. Regularly reading Scripture in the workplace acknowledges God's supremacy, refreshes staff, and reaffirms the foundation of truth your organization rests upon.

Each year, we discern a theme verse for our organization. It points to Christ and highlights a current spiritual emphasis within our ministry. We select a brief phrase from the verse as the name of our annual fund, and it's highlighted in our print materials all year long.

When we're renovating buildings, it's our custom to write out significant verses on the floors before they're carpeted. Each staffer who will serve in that building chooses a handful of Scriptures that pertains to his or her aspect of the ministry, and we join together with Sharpies to lay a bedrock of truth under our feet.

> Forever, O Lord, your word
> is firmly fixed in the heavens.…
> Your word is a lamp to my feet
> and a light to my path.…
> I rejoice at your word
> like one who finds great spoil.
> —Psalm 119:89, 105, 162

4. Pray with your teams.

One of the best ways to honor Christ is to talk with Him. When your teams pull together for meetings, ask someone to open in prayer, or invite several people to pray as they're led. Jesus is in our midst, and when we engage with Him, we acknowledge that He is Lord of our organization.

As we express our adoration, our appreciation for His faithfulness, and our need for His guidance, we are elevating Christ to the proper place in our ministry. Plus, we're encouraged by our co-workers' heartfelt prayers. Meetings are filled with God's presence and the assurance of His ongoing direction.

> "Where two or three are gathered in my name, there am I among them."
> —Matthew 18:20

5. Join together in musical worship.

You may decide to have a weekly, biweekly, or monthly gathering in which honoring the Lord includes musical worship. Try listening quietly to music with lyrics that glorify God, watching a worshipful YouTube video, or passing out song sheets and singing along with a worship song. Music truly is a universal language, and most believers will welcome a time of reorienting themselves to the Lord through it.

You may choose to worship with just one song that corresponds to a scriptural focus, or you may be led to incorporate several songs. Ponder it before the Lord and see how He leads.

> … speaking to one another in psalms and hymns and spiritual songs, singing and making melody in your heart to the Lord.
> —Ephesians 5:19 NKJV

6. Model honor.

Once you've fostered a culture of honor in your business, church, or ministry, you can be tempted to let the "machinery" run on its own. But even machines need to be maintained, and a holy God deserves your active participation in honoring Him. Stay involved and keep leading.

As much as this culture has permeated my life and soul, I can still get tripped up by deadlines and the weight of responsibility. When that happens, it's natural to want to skip out on scheduled worship or prayer. Missing these times occasionally is fine, but remember that your engagement goes a long way in upholding the corporate value of honoring God.

> Let us consider how to stir up one another to love and good
> works, not neglecting to meet together ...
> but encouraging one another.
> —Hebrews 10:24–25

Let God shape a unique culture of honor within your organization. There's no set pattern and no prescribed ingredients; the main component is your desire is to magnify the Lord. As you keep exalting God in these various ways, He will confirm certain activities you've embarked on and lead you into brand-new ones. We're decades into our journey, and God continues to refresh and deepen the ways we honor Him.

It's tempting to codify new practices that begin with lots of energy and vitality. We humans want to hold on to something that works well. But if we cling to it too long or too tightly, we can squeeze the life right out of it. Resist that temptation, allowing God's Spirit to form, reform, and transform your culture as the months and years go by. God has plenty of "fresh wine" and will lead you into new, creative ways to genuinely honor Him.

As God deepens a culture of honor within your organization, He may point out ways in which you've become so focused on your mission that you've lost sight of the Person behind it.

For instance, as a pro-life ministry, we can have a laser beam focus on saving babies and pointing women and men to the Lord.

While these are worthy pursuits, we've learned to view them in the larger context of God's honor. God created humans in His image so they would be born, come to know Him, grow to be His disciples, and live their lives for Him—so that He would receive glory. In other words, it all starts and ends with God.

Think that through in your own mission. See if you're putting a magnifying glass on key aspects of what you've been called to do. If you were to take away the magnifying glass and take in the fullness of God's worthiness, how might your focus and approaches change to become more God-centered and God-honoring?

When a culture of honoring God matures, it becomes systemic. At our ministry, it's evident in every large gathering, in our communication to broader constituents, and in every interaction among our board and staff.

As honoring God becomes established within your organization, spread the word. Tell business associates, fellow pastors, or ministry partners what's going on. Don't overstate it or take credit for it, but don't hide it under a bushel basket either. We're all called to honor God, and your group can be a city on a hill to encourage others to do the same.

A year or so into our new culture, we began sharing it in our newsletters and at our annual banquets. It resonated with financial partners, some of whom became key intercessors for us or members of our staff. At first they learned from afar; then they began putting it into practice in their own lives. When they were led to join us on staff, they were already schooled in the culture, and they entered right into it. Also, many of our partners support our ministry because they know we honor God and follow His lead.

Honoring God must be paramount throughout our organizations, because God is paramount.

I started this chapter by sharing how Ron and I pursued and became fascinated with common loons, to the point of feeling a sense of honor toward them.

As you cultivate honor toward our most uncommon Lord, you will not only be aligned with God; you will become increasingly fascinated with and strengthened by the greatness of who He is.

CHAPTER SEVEN

Everyday Reverence

I entered the blogosphere kicking and screaming.

I knew God wanted me to write a book for leaders about seeking Him with their teams. But I didn't know publishing a book meant I had to delve into all things social media—something I'd proudly and naively avoided for years. So after I started working on this book, I slogged into the unfamiliar Land of Blog.

Ugh. Grrrr. Blech.

In the midst of all this, we had our weekly time of corporate worship at work. The staff member in charge handed each of us one of several Scripture verses she'd found meaningful. She shared the ups and downs of her health journey and how God brought her to a place of surrender. Then she encouraged us to reflect on the verse we'd received and see how God might speak to us through it.

My verse was, "… casting all your anxieties on him, because he cares for you" (1 Peter 5:7). It didn't leap off the page, and I heard no still, small voice. We were invited to share how the verse impacted us, and some people did. I tucked the piece of paper in my Bible.

The next morning, I pulled out my verse and read it in context. God used the verses before it—1 Peter 5:2–3—to speak to me about blogging. Peter was urging leaders to shepherd their flocks willingly, eagerly, and by being an example. As I absorbed those verses and pondered their meaning, I realized God was calling me to blog willingly, eagerly, sharing examples from my own travails and triumphs.

And boom. Just like that, blogging left the obligatory realm and entered the obedience realm. This made a world of difference for me. I found a new purpose in writing blogs, and it's become one of my most enjoyable ventures.

God used our ministry's time of honoring Him to shift my perspective on blogging.

That's the thing about elevating God in your workplace. In addition to bringing Him glory, honoring God leads to

- encountering God, which leads to …
- knowing Him better, which leads to …
- personal transformation, which leads to …
- loving God more, which naturally makes you want to …
- honor Him more.

It's an ever-deepening cycle.

Tools for the Journey

As you begin to revere God in your work setting, you'll need a few tools. Here are ones we use regularly.

Bibles

I've brought my Bible to work every day since a good friend told me, "I take my Sword with me everywhere." It's a rare day at the office that I don't need it and read it. You'll want to have spare Bibles available for times when others may not have theirs, or their smartphones, handy.

Journals, tablets, pens

As in your personal times with the Lord, when you corporately exalt God, He may give you an insight or bring to mind a Scripture verse you'll want to jot down. Keep plenty of paper and pens on hand for everyone to use.

Great worship songs

Stay current by streaming worship music through YouTube, Pandora, iTunes, and so on. Gather an assortment of songs—some that are well-known and easy to sing; quieter, reflective songs; and instrumental background music.

Computers, smartphones, speakers

Most offices have computers and most staffers have a smartphone. Worship music is readily accessible through YouTube and iTunes. Investing in wireless or Bluetooth speakers is wise for larger rooms. We've also purchased quality A/V equipment for large staff gatherings.

Craft supplies

Nothing fancy needed. Just a supply of magic markers, colored pencils, construction paper, scissors, glue—things you may already have at the office. As we learned to magnify God, we grew in expressing our devotion through simple creative projects.

Putting the Tools to Work

So how do we use these tools?

Board meetings, leadership team meetings, and department meetings

The example I'll use in this section is from our leadership team meetings. It's applicable to any meeting where two to twelve people are present.

There are currently five individuals at our biweekly leadership team meetings—myself, our executive vice president, and two vice presidents. The fifth is Jesus. (Just to reinforce this reality!) Because Jesus is present with us as God of the universe and leader of our ministry, we start these two-hour meetings with a time of honoring Him.

While I, as president, facilitate the overall flow of the meeting, we take turns leading our time with God. As this notion of honoring the Lord took root in our ministry, I knew I didn't have a corner on the market when it came to intimacy with God. Although I wanted to champion and model a culture of honor, I knew I shouldn't always be in the driver's seat. That would dishonor other staffers, narrow our worship, and limit the insights we could glean through each other's connection with God. Each member of the leadership team has a strong relationship with Jesus and is well able to lead us in a time of engaging with Him.

Since God is magnificent and beyond understanding, it can seem difficult to honor Him sufficiently. Instead of trying to magnify all of His multifaceted greatness, we sometimes zero in on individual aspects of His character. The leader may choose an attribute of God and share why it's been meaningful to him or her. The rest of us enter in, reflecting on that characteristic and sharing personally. We may worship together with a related song and then pray together.

These initial twenty to thirty minutes set the tone for the rest of our meeting. As we talked about in chapter 5, honoring lordship brings alignment. When our leadership team acknowledges

God's preeminence, we become aligned with Him, and His wisdom is available for the discussions and decisions throughout the meeting. God's wisdom is always available, of course, but we're not always attuned to Him. Exalting God heightens our awareness of His presence and wisdom.

As you contemplate this paradigm for your board meetings, leadership team meetings, and department meetings, picture Jesus in your midst. Think about ways you can corporately elevate Him. Think simple. Think creative. Think outside the box. It's not necessarily a typical devotion in which one person shares Scripture and offers a mini teaching. It's more a time when everyone is leaning close and peering at a wonderful aspect of God. Remember to rotate leadership. Here are some ways to honor the Lord.

- Choose one Scripture verse that's impacted you recently, make copies of it for everyone, and pass them around. Share how the verse has enhanced your view of God, and invite others to do the same. If your team is larger, you might choose a separate verse for each person to add variety.

- Select an attribute of God—such as faithfulness or sovereignty—and talk together about how you've seen that aspect of God's character demonstrated in your church, ministry, or business.

- Ask people to share a recent example, within your common mission, of where they've seen God at work.

Watch a YouTube music video or listen to a song that relates to the characteristic of God you've reflected on. Sing together, and then pray together. Be flexible and be led by the Spirit. You can engage in these activities in any order and for any length of time.

Headquarters worship

At our headquarters building, where a dozen or so staff members serve, we gather weekly to honor God. While there are several departments working together in the same building, we all serve the same God and we want to lift Him up as a group.

For this gathering, there's a bit more time to be with God—a full hour. We currently meet at 9:00 on Monday mornings to start the week with God at the forefront. In the past, we've met at 11:00 and paired the meeting with lunch to give staffers a longer break from work.

As with leadership team meetings, we invite each staffer to take a turn leading. We don't require this, not wanting anyone to feel constrained to lead. Even in a group of people who know each other fairly well, it can be daunting to guide your peers and supervisors in a time of seeking God. Sometimes it takes new staffers a while to feel comfortable facilitating, but usually before long they take a turn.

We don't ask the leader to provide a devotion or time of teaching. Rather, we invite him or her to steer us through an exercise that will help us individually and corporately connect with God. Here are some examples.

- In one case, the staffer in charge emailed us early that morning, inviting us to take a walk outside at 11:00 to look for evidences of God. At her direction, we each spent a half hour walking or sitting quietly and taking in the sights and sounds. When we gathered afterward, some of us brought wildflowers, and others brought crazy tales of creepy critters observed. We laughed together and shared the various ways our experiences in nature drew our focus to God.

- Another time, the leader handed each person a passage of Scripture with one of the seven "I Am" statements from the gospel of John. "I am ... the bread of life, the light of the world, the gate." We were invited to meditate on our passage and write a haiku to convey its meaning. Haikus are brief poems consisting of three short lines with a certain number of syllables in each. The first line has five syllables, the second has seven, and the third has five. They're easy to write, and they help you engage with Scripture in a fresh way. When we finished our poems, we had the opportunity to read them to the group.

  Here's a Haiku based on John 6:35: "Jesus said to them, 'I am the bread of life; whoever comes to me shall not hunger, and whoever believes in me shall never thirst.'"

  > You nourish me, Lord
  > You are spiritual food
  > Sustaining my soul

- One time, we entered our worship room to find craft items strewn across the floor. The leader gave each of us a phrase from Hebrews 1 that described Jesus' character or accomplishments. Everyone was invited to meditate on their phrase, think about how it exemplified Jesus, and illustrate it on a large piece of card stock. People shared their phrase and what it meant to them, and we strung together the illustrations to make a mobile for the room.

As you can imagine, these times are invaluable. Amazing things happen when a group of people step out of the pressures of work and into a place set aside to meet with God. It's a place where staffers can just be. And breathe. And drink in God's greatness. And

101

create. And express. And take in Scripture. And worship. And in the process of honoring God, become replenished.

A waste of time? Far from it. Ask God, who is honored and enjoying our fellowship. Ask our staff, who is experiencing regular refreshment and increased productivity.

Branch locations

At our ministry, we have several facilities for serving clients, each staffed separately. We encourage the director of each location to seek the Lord's leading in how his or her particular teams honor God. On any given day, small teams of volunteers are present to minister to clients, and the director meets with them at the beginning of the shift for a time of worship and prayer.

Here's one director's description:

"Our worship and prayer times before each shift feel like mini church meetings. Volunteers are from varied church backgrounds, but we're united in our love for Jesus and our desire to serve Him. The gatherings are led by a volunteer, another staff member, or myself as director. As God leads, sometimes we share personal praises and prayer, sometimes we read Scripture and pray, and sometimes we worship. As we set aside the busyness of the day and join in seeking His face, we are empowered to go into the education rooms and serve our clients well."

Another director adds:

"The goal is always to share something that inspires us toward God's greatness and His love for us and our clients. And also to pray together—especially that God prepares hearts for the gospel. But sometimes circumstances will dictate flexibility. Perhaps a volunteer comes in with a burden needing immediate attention, or there may be a phone call or a walk-in client that takes priority. When this happens, we go with it and trust that God's grace will cover us."

And another:

"I focus on the themes the Lord has been speaking to me personally, so that I am 'pouring out' what the Lord has 'poured into' me. God is faithful to continually provide new and encouraging words of truth to share. Before we pray, as time allows, I always open it up for volunteers to share what God is saying to them about the topic as well. Over the years, I have had numerous volunteers tell me how much those times mean to them. One stated, 'It sets the tone for the whole day and beyond!'"

Full-staff meetings

Our staff meets monthly for varying purposes and amounts of time. Typically, meetings are three hours long and include thirty to forty-five minutes set apart specifically for God. Again, we invite staffers to lead. Since there's no set way to worship God, we encourage them to be creative as they discern how to lead. Our worship times have included things like:

- live worship music with a guitar or keyboard
- an artist who unveiled her paintings one at a time while we reflected on how they portrayed God
- a meaningful story, read out loud
- someone gifted in God-honoring dance
- a gospel-focused illusionist

They've also featured a playlist of worship YouTube videos with lyrics.

Once or twice a year, we spend a full day together as staff. We devote the day to drawing near to God and learning more about

Him. This time is usually led by someone on our leadership team; occasionally, it's led by a local pastor or ministry leader. We focus on an aspect of God's character or an insight from Scripture that's prominent in our ministry at the time. These are rich, unifying days, keeping everyone in step with the current thrust of God's heart for our ministry.

Personal days with God

Several times a year, we pay our staff members to take the day away from the office and spend it with God. We provide guidelines for their time but allow plenty of freedom so they can follow God's leading. The day may include Bible reading, prayer, journaling, walking outside, going to a park, sitting by a lake, getting together with a friend—whatever enables the staff member to refocus and refuel in the Lord.

Of everything we've incorporated into our culture of honoring God, this feature is perhaps most appreciated by our staff. There's something about being paid to be with God that enhances the intentionality and significance of the day. Our staff members view it as a gift, they cherish the time, and because of it, they've grown deeper in their walk with the Lord. We've found that the spiritual impact on our staffers circles back and blesses our ministry. This is the heart and wisdom of God. He wants to pour more of Himself into us so we can pour more of Him into our work and the people we're serving.

Getting Started

1. Cast the vision

As I mentioned in the previous chapter, it's important for you to share with your staff how and why you've become convicted about corporately honoring God. Let them in on your personal growth and why you believe elevating God will bless Him, replenish everyone in the organization, and advance your mission.

2. Plan how to honor God together

As you determine where to implement corporate honor in your work setting, look for natural groupings of individuals. Departments are the most obvious, but if they're too large, look for smaller teams within those departments. Also, plan a regular time for the whole team in your facility to meet together for worship. And if you have several facilities and periodic full-staff meetings, that's a great time to corporately acknowledge and exalt God.

3. Start slowly

Resist the temptation to map out for your team(s) a whole new scenario that may feel overwhelming. Begin with the team you believe will be most receptive—probably your key associates. Take time seeking God with them, and then follow God's timing in branching out with other teams and eventually your full staff. Also, discern when to share your vision with your board and invite them to consider more actively honoring God at their meetings.

4. Invite feedback

Let your staff know you desire an open dialogue about their responses to your corporate time with God. Listen to their affirmations and hesitations. Tweak the activities as needed, without giving up your commitment to honor the Lord.

5. Be patient with naysayers

Remember any resistance you felt as you read this book, and realize that some staffers may have a natural reticence to spending work time this way. Encourage them to participate, without pressuring them to engage verbally. Give them time to acclimate.

6. Make adjustments

Sometimes naysayers or nonparticipants are shedding light on an aspect of your culture that has grown cold or stale. Be attuned to their feedback, and be open to God's leading in new ways of honoring Him.

7. Keep it fresh and alive

There are limitless ways to give God glory, and we can easily fall into our favorite ruts. Inviting others to take the lead and encouraging them to be creative will reveal fresh avenues for exalting Him.

Honoring God could easily be the end-all. But it's not. In His bigheartedness, God not only wants a thriving relationship with us; He also wants us to have healthy relationships with one another. What He's really after is family. He's our Father and we're His children. Like any loving dad, God wants to have a great relationship with His kids, and He wants them to love each other.

CHAPTER EIGHT

Agreement

"I've been getting the impression from God that we should fast from our morning worship times, Lisa."

To me, this was both sacrilegious and preposterous. But it came from a trusted long-term associate, Kati, and it gave me pause.

Our headquarters' staffers had been worshiping for the first hour of every workday for ten years, and while some of them had grown tired of it, I still found great value in those times with the Lord. Kati and I were aware of the disengaged staffers and had discussed and prayed about ways to reinvigorate them.

Back then, our times of honoring God were composed of musical worship followed by ten to fifteen minutes of prayer. We'd embraced the concept of worshiping before an "audience of one," so even though there were seven or eight of us, we basically worshiped individually. Kati and I were often the only ones who prayed. We thought if we prayed longer and harder, others would catch on. When that didn't work, we pulled back from praying as much, hoping others would step up. That didn't work either. The silence wasn't golden.

We decided to discuss it with the group. They suggested methods to vary the ways we connected with God, and we tried them. But to no avail. It seemed like the end of an era.

Even so, I hung on for weeks. I clung to those morning worship times much as I'd clung to our times of prayer for clients ten years prior. I remembered how God had to wrest that routine from my hands as well.

But still, fast from worship? Who does that? Isn't God always worthy? What if we lose the God-honoring ground we've gained?

It all felt too risky to me.

Yet God had His way. I eventually saw the wisdom of taking a break, and Kati and I declared a three-month "worship fast," with the caveat that we would all come together for worship whenever anyone felt led. And every week or so someone did. Kati and I kept track of how often we gathered in this Spirit-prompted way, and we agreed there was more life in those occasions.

What we didn't know then was that God had removed worship for a season so He could usher in another aspect of the paradigm—relational community. Our worship had greatly enhanced our relationship with God, but our relationships with one another had remained static. Aside from praying for one another occasionally, we hadn't pressed into knowing each other more deeply.

But isn't God always worthy of worship?

Yes, He is. But as I said at the close of the last chapter, He's a Father. As believers, we're His children. And He designed all of us to relate and function together as members of His family.

Who knew!

Well, obviously, God knew all along. He made it perfectly clear through Jesus' answer to the Pharisee's question about the greatest commandment.

Jesus said that the first and greatest commandment was to "Love the Lord your God with all your heart and with all your soul and with all your mind" (Matt. 22:37 NIV). Then, without slowing down, He rolled right into the next one, saying, "And the second is like it: 'Love your neighbor as yourself'" (v. 39 NIV).

Those greatest commandments were forever elevated and paired when Jesus added, "All the Law and the Prophets hang on these two commandments" (v. 40 NIV).

Jesus was saying that the Old Testament found its fulfillment in Him and in the new kingdom life He instituted—a life characterized by family-style love. Because of Jesus' life and death and resurrection, we can have a full-fledged love relationship with our heavenly Father, and loving relationships with the people in our lives.

Now, these aren't earthshaking concepts to any of us. Not unless you bring them into the work setting.

Think about it. What if the relationships in our churches, businesses, and ministries were characterized by a biblical version of family-style love? Picture the unity, the harmony, the potential for agreement.

You may be saying, "Yeah, but picture the messiness. Family dynamics aren't neat and tidy, like office cubicles!" I agree, and we'll get to that. But for now, let's wrap our minds around at-work, family-style love that leads to a group of people experiencing deeper agreement with God and with one another.

That's the second principle of the productive pause:

Cultivating relationships brings agreement.

Agreement isn't just a compliant nod of the head or a militaristic lineup. It's a multidimensional harmony characterized by close relationships, a shared sense of mission, a tapestry of perspectives and opinions, and a mutual commitment to move forward with God.

This harmony is the polar opposite of a Gregorian chant. It's the opposite of a drummer setting the beat and expecting everyone to march in lockstep. Rather it's each team member's gifting, viewpoint, and insight welcomed by leadership and laid before the Lord, who uses it all to sound a glorious clarion call directing the organization to advance.

And agreement doesn't happen overnight. It follows weeks, months, sometimes years of growing together in loving God and loving one another.

For instance, consider the statement "We agreed to move Mother to a retirement home." Anyone with aging parents will know that the siblings and spouses didn't stumble upon that decision while savoring English sticky toffee pudding one evening.

No, agreement is a pregnant concept, full of hearty discussions, diverse opinions, raw honesty, awkwardness, conflict, and incremental gains in trust and love. And as with pregnancy, agreement births something new. For churches, ministries, and businesses, agreement produces new decisions, new emphases, new vision.

Breaking It Down

Let's look at the complete principle and break it down section by section.

Because God is our Father and we are His sons and daughters, we love Him wholeheartedly and cultivate authentic, loving relationships with one another. This brings agreement.

1. *"Because God is our Father and we are His sons and daughters ...*

Clearly, these words portray family.

The New Testament describes the church through a variety of metaphors—the body of Christ, the bride of Christ, the flock, the temple, and the family of God. Of all these, the metaphor of God's family is most pervasive.

Scripture is filled with references to God as our Father and to us as His children.

See what great love the Father has lavished on us,
that we should be called children of God!
And that is what we are!

—1 John 3:1 NIV

I will be a father to you, and you shall be sons and daughters to
me, says the Lord Almighty.

—2 Corinthians 6:18

Now you Gentiles are no longer strangers and foreigners.
You are citizens along with all of God's holy people.
You are members of God's family.

—Ephesians 2:19 NLT

Functioning as the family of God in your church, business, or ministry is a higher calling spiritually than simply being a group of staff members. Granted, there are similarities—in both cases, there are leaders, members, relationships, and functions. But the biblical understanding of God's family is worth noting and implementing in the work environment.

A Heavenly Father

The predominant character in this family is God Himself. He has a father's heart toward us. He is for us, He understands us, He wants us to succeed. Ultimately, He wants us to be like Him.

The Greek word for father, *patér,* conveys one who both imparts life and is committed to it, one who has an intimate connection with his children, a progenitor who brings offspring into existence in order to pass on the potential for likeness (HELPS Word-studies).

Simply said, our heavenly Father grants us physical and spiritual life, fosters a close relationship with us, and is dedicated to helping us become like Him.

Can you see how this reality forms the bedrock of confidence on which we live our lives and work at our jobs? We have a heavenly Father who loves us, and He is the one we're serving.

Sons and Daughters

When we come into a relationship with God through Jesus, we're adopted into God's family. Our identity is rooted in the unchanging, everlasting truth that God is our Father and we are His children.

A child in the Greek, *tekna,* is figuratively anyone living in full dependence on the heavenly Father, drawing guidance, care, and nurture from Him and willingly submitting to His plan. This is how God transforms that person into His likeness.

Additionally, the Greek words for son, *huious*, and daughter, *thygateras*, emphasize that we share the same nature as our Father and are able to reflect His character more and more as we live in faith.

Do you see the thread of thought here? The Father wants us to become like Him, and as God's children, we're empowered by Him to do just that!

As Christians in the workplace, we often derive our identity from the position we hold and the job we do. But these things are transient. A child of God derives his identity from God Himself, which is a permanent relationship. And he's designed to increasingly exhibit his Father's traits. When these truths become our reality, we function in loving faithfulness and productivity unto God.

Brothers and Sisters

Having a vertical relationship with our heavenly Father puts us in a horizontal relationship with each other, as siblings—brothers and sisters in Christ.

Scripture writers used terms like brothers and sisters because we can relate to this concept in the natural realm. Siblings live, chow down, build forts, belly laugh, and scuffle together. (I have, and have given, the scars to prove it!) That's why there are so many New Testament verses about getting along and loving each other. For example:

> Live in harmony with one another.
> —Romans 12:16 NIV

Love one another.
—John 13:34 NIV

Confess your faults one to another.
—James 5:16 KJV

"She started it, Dad!" Yep, spiritual brothers and sisters have a lot to learn when it comes to living in harmony with each other. But it's a journey worth pursuing. It leads to deeper, more honest relationships on the job, enabling us to glean from varied opinions and move forward in agreement.

Growing in Christlikeness

As we live as brothers and sisters in authentic, loving relationships, our goal is to point each other toward Christ. "Those God foreknew he also predestined to be conformed to the image of his Son, that he might be the firstborn among many brothers and sisters" (Rom. 8:29 NIV).

When we share openly with one another in a work setting, it's not solely so we can vent. It's so we can help each other become more like our older brother, Jesus Christ. As staffers grow in Christlikeness, organizations grow in cohesion and effectiveness, and reflect more of God's glory.

On Mission Together

Since we're members of God's household, we're about our Father's business, just like Jesus was (Luke 2:49). Our Father sets the overarching vision and mission of our organizations, and we, as a family, pursue it with Him.

Sometimes in churches, ministries, and businesses, the mission is king and the staff members are its subjects. Not so in the kingdom of God. There the Father is King and we're His children. In the Father's family, love reigns, relationships are real, conversations are robust, and agreement can be reached. Mission accomplished—family-style.

One of the most intense conversations we've had with our board and leadership team concerned a decision about whether to move forward with a public hearing. An action had been levied against our ministry, and Christian legislators and lawyers believed it warranted a hearing. They felt that taking the issue to court would uphold religious freedom. The pros and cons were plentiful, as were the Scripture verses that seemed to substantiate either position. Interestingly, the constant throughout all the prayer and discussion was the lack of peace about moving forward. Eventually, we all leaned toward not participating in the hearing.

As brothers and sisters wanting to follow our heavenly Father's will, none of us had an agenda or dug in our heels. We all had a surrendered posture toward the Father and an honoring posture toward each other as we pressed forward to seek understanding. And we maintained that posture even when strong opinions were expressed. In the end, we were drawn closer to one another for having grappled with a high-stakes decision as members of God's family.

2. "… we love Him wholeheartedly …"

In the previous three chapters, we learned how honoring lordship brings alignment. You may wonder how honor and love are different. Let's compare the two in the original language.

As we said, honor means to make weighty, magnify, glorify, prize, value, revere.

Honor is a sense of awe and amazement at the grandeur of God. It's also a sense of our humanness and sinfulness. When we honor God, we're acknowledging His infinite greatness, and we're aware of our own finiteness.

In contrast, love means to affectionately adore, steadfastly cleave to, take pleasure in, long for, promptly obey, and show a discriminating affection for, which involves choice and selection.

If a physical posture for honor is standing with arms extended to the heavens and with a look of wonder on our face, then a posture for love would be engaging in a heartfelt embrace with a look of contentment.

When you ponder the meaning of those Greek phrases for love, you quickly realize that loving God is not for the faint of heart! If it weren't for the fact that "we love him, because he first loved us" (1 John 4:19 KJV), we'd be hopelessly unable to love God the way He deserves.

But thankfully, God is love (1 John 4:16). Using the noun form of love in the Greek, we could say that God is affection, God is goodwill, God is benevolence, God is esteem. There's also a strong sense of preference in the meaning of the Greek word. God prefers us. He chose us before the foundations of the world.

So picture this God who has loved and chosen you since before time began, who gave His Son's life for you, and who runs to hug you and throw a party for you when you return to Him.

How do you respond to that kind of love!

You respond in kind.

Scripture says we're to love God with our whole heart, soul, and mind. That means we cultivate a deep affection for God, the kind of affection a son or daughter feels toward their dad. We long to be in His presence and want to spend time with Him. We're committed to obey Him, realizing He knows best and is trustworthy. And we think about Him often, meditating on truths about Him from His Word.

One of our former staffers, Carol, described it this way:

"Having an awareness of God with me—all the time—entreats me to communicate with Him about anything and everything, anytime. I don't need to stop everything just so I can summon up emotions of closeness or love for God. How I love and crave those necessary times of just Him and me, but even when I meet with a client, interact with coworkers, or step outside to breathe in some fresh air, I experience intimacy with God as my soul and spirit call out, 'Abba, Father' in praise and petition."

3. "… we cultivate authentic, loving relationships with one another"

As we stated at the outset of this chapter, loving God and loving one another are the two greatest commandments. When I think about how we're even able to obey these commandments, I picture it in this sequence:

1. God lavishes His love on us.
2. We receive His love and respond by loving Him back.
3. We love ourselves in agreement with His love for us.
4. We love others with the love He's given us.

It's easy to view these forms of love as givens. We think, *Of course God loves us (yawn). And, yes, we love Him too (snore).*

And I guess we're supposed to love ourselves (whatever that means). And, oh yes, we should certainly have a loving attitude toward others (ho hum).

Many of us have heard these admonitions since Sunday school. But do we actually love? And do we intentionally love the people we work with?

What if we took the time to ask about a coworker's family? What if we remembered to ask how their sick child is doing? What if we spent a few minutes in department meetings sharing something God has been teaching us? What if we shared an area we're struggling in? What if we each prayed for the person on our right, all around the circle? What if we lovingly called out a coworker on an area they've been slipping in? What if someone loved us enough to be honest with us about something like that?

Hmmm … what if love includes iron sharpening iron?

In our early days of serving in ministry together, Kati and I decided we didn't like the phrase "iron sharpens iron." So to describe our relationship, we coined the phrase "velvet softens velvet." Back then, our relationship consisted of affection, admiration, respect, encouragement, and positive feedback. We were each other's fans, and we liked it that way.

The problem was, we weren't in heaven yet, and we both had our share of burrs and rough spots! Plus, there's a certain dullness that settles into a relationship made solely of kudos. And who's in a better position to give you accurate feedback than someone who sees you at your best and worst all week long? They see what makes you bristle in meetings, how you respond to stress, and where your work style needs work.

Agreement

Wounds from a friend can be trusted.

—Proverbs 27:6 NIV

Not long after we discontinued our daily hour of worship at the ministry, Kati approached me with a desire to go deeper in our relationship. She'd begun attending a church where people were encouraged to be gut-level real with one another, for the purpose of building up each other in Christ. She had entered into that, had experienced its benefits, and wanted the same for our relationship.

I was initially put off by the inference that our relationship was lacking. And to be honest, I wasn't so sure I wanted Kati knowing the real me. What if she gave me feedback I didn't want to hear? What if we didn't like each other anymore? And besides, I was her boss. Wasn't there some boundary we shouldn't cross?

(If you think you're detecting a pattern in me, you're right. I can chafe at new ideas at first, especially when they're not my own! Thankfully, before too long God graces me to see His wisdom, recognize that He's using others to lead me, and follow that leading. You may be the same way. Leaders like to lead, and they want to be sure they've accurately sensed God's direction. But good leaders also follow. So if you've felt resistance toward the concepts in this book, hang in there. Chances are, God is speaking to your heart. If you let Him, He'll nudge you in His direction.)

Kati and I took the plunge, and we haven't looked back.

And wondrously, God has spread the concept of relational community throughout our ministry. We're still learning and working out very real kinks, but it's become a staple of our culture. It's also the key to coming into agreement with God and one another, so our mission can advance.

CHAPTER NINE

Love Takes Action

It was early evening and the river was calm. A perfect time to be out on the water. Ron and I paddled our kayaks past our neighbor's dock, where a mallard duck was squawking her head off. "That's odd," I said to Ron. "There's nothing there but a dock, and she's throwing a fit."

I wouldn't have thought of it again, but when we came back an hour later, she was still there making a ruckus.

I ventured closer. She reluctantly back-paddled but intensified her quacks. That's when I heard the faint squeaks.

All at once I realized what happened.

"Oh my word, Ron! There are ducklings under the dock! I can hear them. They must've gotten swept underneath by the trough of a wake."

"What?" Ron said, with bewilderment.

But sure enough, when Ron pulled his kayak against the dock, he heard the peeping sounds for himself. He peered through the slots and saw five tiny fluffballs paddling around frantically.

"We have to rescue them!" I said. "They're trapped, and there's no way they'll be able to dive underwater to escape. They'll starve or become pike food!"

Ever up for a challenge, Ron beat me back to our cottage, and we devised our plan in whispered tones. Our neighbors hadn't yet returned for the season, and messing with their dock felt a little devious.

We would use a hammer and crowbar to pry off a side board, and then we'd lure the ducklings out with pieces of bread. Ron ran to the shed; I ran to the kitchen.

Tools in hand, we crept onto our neighbor's dock and sent the mother duck into another conniption. Ron found a loose board and had it off in seconds. I started dropping bread cubes at the opening.

Nothing. The ducklings stayed at the end of the dock, near their mother's voice.

"Oh shoot!" I said to Ron. "How are we going to get them to come out?"

Neither of us knew, so we waited.

Suddenly, one baby duck popped through the opening. Then another and another. None touched the bread; they seemed drawn by the shaft of light. The mother spied them and zipped over, calling loudly to the others. Four. Five. They were all out.

And off they went, without a word of appreciation, happily floating downriver.

Their reunion was all the thanks we needed. We replaced the board and walked home, our heroes' hearts swelling.

Love takes action.

Whether it's rescuing wildlife, reining in wild kids, or grappling with a wild scenario with a few staffers at work, love does something about it. It moves in with good intentions. It moves toward others.

That's the kind of love within the Trinity. God invites us to love Him and one another with this same type of love.

So as we talk about wholeheartedly loving God and each other in the workplace, let's dig a little deeper into this concept of towardness.

The Greek word translated as "with" in John 1:1–2 actually means "toward." In this passage, Jesus is described as the Word who, in the beginning, was God and was with God—that is, toward Him as we discussed in chapter 4.

We know that the Father, Son, and Spirit were present at creation, but we sometimes picture them simply being together and carrying out their roles in a coordinated fashion. Working side by side, so to speak.

But "toward" conveys a far more intentional pursuit of the other. It's a desire to move nearer to the other person, to be together, up close. The Trinity's relational posture is one of face-to-face love, honor, interaction, intimacy.

Think of the towardness demonstrated at Jesus' baptism, when the Father bent down from heaven, bellowing His approval: "This is My beloved Son, in whom I am well pleased" (Matt. 3:17 NKJV).

Or the deference Jesus demonstrated as He said to the Father, "Not My will, but Yours" (Luke 22:42 NKJV).

Or the honor Jesus gave the Spirit when He told the disciples it was better that He was going to the Father, because they'd have the Spirit within them.

For a vivid picture of how God moves toward His children, read Psalm 18:7–19, where He opens the heavens and comes down to rescue David. And us.

What's unfathomable but true is that God not only rescues us but invites us into the intimate oneness the Trinity enjoys. Jesus prays in John 17 that we will be one, just as He and the Father are one, and that we'll experience the love they share.

We have an open invitation to reciprocate.

What does it look like to intentionally love God—move toward Him—on any given workday?

At our ministry, we've compiled a list to encourage staffers to foster intimacy with God as we walk with Him through the work-week. I shared part of it in chapter 5. Here are a few more ways to draw near to Him.

1. Pull your chair away from your desk, face a window if possible, and be still and know that He is God.

2. Stop what you're doing, turn your attention to God, and take a few minutes to express your love to Him for who He is. Then thank Him for what He's doing in your life.

3. Push aside whatever you're working on, get a blank piece of paper, find a few colored markers, and creatively illustrate what God means to you today.

4. Pull up a worship song on your computer or phone and engage with God through adoration and praise.

5. Open your Bible or journal and continue the conversation you were having with God that morning.

Do these simple acts of moving toward God make a difference? Absolutely. Here's how Heather, a long-term staffer, describes it:

"There is a keen awareness of God's omnipresence when I make the time to connect with Him throughout my workday. To experience the Father's love and acknowledge His desire to be involved in every moment of my day brings me to a place of surrender and trust. There is a sense of rest that settles into the deepest part of my being because I know that the God of the universe is here to delight in me and I in Him. There is an intimacy that is created in these moments that deepens our love relationship and brings much joy!"

Not only does God want us to move toward Him, He also wants us to move toward others. So much so that the Greek word translated as "one another," *allelon,* is used one hundred times in the New Testament. *Allelon* conveys a mutual and reciprocal action from one believer toward another. Fifty-nine of these uses are in direct commands about how we should relate to each other. Let's take a look at the breakdown.

- Seventeen of the commands are about loving one another.
- Seventeen involve a direct action, such as serving, forgiving, living in harmony.
- Ten are about edifying each other in the Lord.
- Nine speak to our heart attitude toward one another.
- Six prohibit specific negative behaviors against others.

How well the Father knows His children! He knows we have a tough time loving each other, so He repeats the command to love seventeen times. He knows we want to pull away from one another because of our differences, so He gives lots of commands about engaging with each other. And He knows we're inclined to think and speak negatively about each other, so He admonishes us about judging and slandering.

If Jesus had made a statement about relationships in the work setting, it might have sounded like this: "In your workplace, you will have trouble and disagreement. But take heart! I'll show you and your team how to gather together and navigate through it."

Key "One Another's" for Building Relational Community in the Work Setting

Of the fifty-nine "one another" commands in the New Testament, four concepts make up the foundation of a culture of relational community.

Honoring One Another

Honor is the bedrock for our understanding of community, because it's an acknowledgement of the image bearer that each person is—a human being created in God's likeness and designed to reflect Him throughout life.

I don't know about you, but I find it difficult to feel honor toward the person who just cut me off on the highway, or the cashier who's busy chatting with her coworker at the grocery store. Not to mention the sharp-tongued relative, or the friend who dominates social gatherings.

But when I look past someone's behavior to see the essence of their identity as an individual—a unique expression of God's creativity—I can choose to honor them.

The same applies to the work setting. Think of the coworkers you've struggled with through the years. Maybe their personalities bug you or they're simply gifted differently from you. Honoring them means choosing to view them as individuals designed by God, with very specific and unique traits.

And as in marriages and families, when God assembles a work team, He seems to delight in putting together people who are vastly different from one another.

This is intentional on God's part. He crafted each of us with unique strengths that have built-in limitations, because He wants us to need each other. There are no superstars in the body of Christ. We each have just a portion of God's giftings, so we're much better together.

At our ministry, one of the ways we honor the God-given uniqueness of each individual on staff is to get to know their giftings, personality traits, and skill sets. We use tools like the Spiritual Gift Survey: Motivating Spiritual Gifts of Grace; Gifts of Grace: The Character of Christ in His People; The DISC Personality System; and StrengthFinders to identify key areas where individuals naturally shine.

While we've found it very helpful to understand each other's bents, we're careful not to pigeonhole one another. Yes, we each have a chief motivating drive, but we're not one-dimensional. Each of us has a unique blend of giftings, strengths, and weaknesses. And we're all called to increased Christlikeness in every area of our lives.

We've also learned that our gifts and skills are complementary. When more gifts are represented around a table and each person is encouraged to share his or her perspective, there is greater discernment and wisdom.

On our leadership team, for instance, we have a visionary, two strategists, and an administrator. A visionary without a strategist is like an Airbus headed to Alaska without a GPS. A strategist without a visionary is like a contractor building a high-rise with no blueprint. An administrator without a visionary and a strategist is like a factory without a product or a production flowchart.

As the visionary on our team, I'm full of ideas. Some of them are good, some not so much. My teammates honor me by considering my latest schemes and by letting me know when they're not feasible or not for now. Steve and Katie B, as we affectionately call her, are our strategists. They know how to map out a plan to make vision reality. They're big-picture, get 'er done types, and we welcome their broad-stroke strategies. When they overlook important details, though, we speak up and fill in the gaps. Kati's our administrator. She's great at knowing the intricacies of coordinating staff manpower to launch a new initiative and often puts the brakes on our timeline. We honor her by heeding her hesitation or by prodding her along if she's overwhelmed by a mountain of details.

I could get hurt when the others don't like my ideas. Steve and Katie B could feel held back when Kati and I remind them about details. And Kati could get frustrated when the rest of us soar off into the stratosphere.

We do get annoyed with one another sometimes. But we understand each other's quirks, we value each other's strengths, and we've learned to celebrate the synergy in our giftings.

Loving One Another

There's nothing chintzy or thin about the caliber of love God asks us to have for one another. God commands us to love each other "earnestly" (1 Peter 4:8) and "more and more" (1 Thess. 4:9–

10). As if those orders weren't tall enough, He also asks us to love one another "just as I have loved you" (John 13:34).

So what does love look like in a work setting? Here are a few ways we seek to love each other at our ministry.

- Greeting one another with sincere friendliness, as an acknowledgement of every person's worth and our desire to be in relationship with each other

- Taking a genuine interest in each other's personal lives, recognizing that we're whole people with lives beyond the ministry

- Opening up about our personal lives, with authenticity and appropriate vulnerability

- Bearing each other's burdens through listening and prayer, freeing hearts and minds to focus on the work at hand

- Sending a welcome card to new staff members and giving them the opportunity to share a little about themselves at staff meetings

- Gathering around staffers in prayer when they leave the ministry, and asking God to prosper them in their next kingdom assignment

- Having lunch together once a week, for light conversation and hearty laughter

- Pairing up to take walks together so we can enjoy the outdoors and get to know one another in a casual setting

- Holding birthday lunches for each other, with a special dessert and a personally-selected rendition of "Happy Birthday" (ranging from "angelic with snorts" to reggae—it's hysterical!)

Relational community also involves the tough version of love that speaks difficult truth. Spending all or most of the day together, we get to know each other's idiosyncrasies, weaknesses, and flaws. And most of us are blind to our own. Who better to hold up a mirror and speak into your life than a trusted comrade?

One of the most loving things a board member did for me was to pull me aside to address how my enthusiasm for a certain doctrinal viewpoint could bring division to our ministry. She didn't critique my position but warned me of the consequences and explained that it wasn't uncommon for ministry leaders to part ways in situations like ours. Her words, pointed but loving, were all it took to rein me back into a more unifying approach.

Edifying One Another

Seeking God together has become, for us, a wellspring of spiritual and relational life. Besides the scheduled times—daily at our service locations, weekly at headquarters, and monthly at board and staff meetings—there's a natural flow of edification between staffers throughout any given day.

Two Scriptures beautifully describe this:

> Let the word of Christ dwell in you richly, teaching
> and admonishing one another in all wisdom,
> singing psalms and hymns and spiritual songs,
> with thankfulness in your hearts to God.
>
> —Colossians 3:16

> Let us consider how to stir up one another to love and good works,
> not neglecting to meet together, as is the habit of some,
> but encouraging one another.
>
> —Hebrews 10:24–25

As members of the body of Christ, we each have a personal relationship with Jesus. Each of us has valuable spiritual insights and life lessons to share, and we can learn from one another's perspectives. We welcome this at our ministry and seek to encourage each other in our relationship with Christ, through conversations, prayer, encouraging emails, and so forth.

Once, in a staff meeting, I was about to introduce and explain the annual theme for our ministry that year. But during worship, I sensed that instead of unpacking the theme myself, I should simply present the concept and invite the staff to prayerfully discern its implications. After several minutes of waiting on the Lord, the staff shared keen insights related to the theme, broadening its implications. At the next meeting, several staff members provided mini-teachings, elaborating on what God had put in their hearts and taking the theme to a deeper level for each of us. We were all edified by the breadth of wisdom shared.

Living in Harmony with One Another

In a perfect world, every staffer is on board with God, with the mission, and with your policy on conflict resolution.

But in the organizational worlds you and I live in, this is seldom the case.

We may assume that staff members will respect authority, share grievances with their supervisor, and work out differences according to Matthew 18, especially if they're believers. But our staffers are also human. And so are we. And humans don't always agree or get along.

A harmonious culture isn't a given, but it is worth fighting for. Here are a few things that will help.

- Intentional time, in bimonthly or monthly meetings, spent developing genuine relationships within departments—time in which both supervisors and those they supervise are being the body of Christ together

- Regular opportunities for staffers to share thoughts, ideas, input, and feedback about the organization (whether or not these pertain to areas in their realm of responsibility), trusting leadership to follow God's leading as they consider the issues

- A shared commitment to honor leadership and proper channels of communication—through which, instead of discussing grievances laterally, staffers express them to their supervisor

It takes time to build a culture of bona fide and safe relational community, but it pays off.

I mentioned the various giftings of our leadership team and the inevitable clashes we've experienced while working together. In the early days, those clashes often went unaddressed as we tried to maintain a semblance of peace. But they'd crop up again and again. As we grew to understand and love each other more, we were able to discuss them within a few days. Eventually, we felt safe enough with one another to deal with conflicts while they were happening. None of us wanted to go through a meeting with our blind spots causing trouble, so we committed to holding up mirrors for each other in the midst of conflict. And now we most often handle issues immediately.

I remember the first time I did this. We were on a conference call because I was working from home. When an unresolved issue erupted, I began pacing in frustration across my family room floor.

Here we go again, I thought. But then I remembered our commitment to honesty in the moment, and I said, "So are you guys feeling the same tension I'm feeling? Let's talk about it." And we did. We sought to understand each other's perspectives, and the result was a decision compiled of several opinions, instead of a stalemated tug-of-war. And wondrously, we felt closer to each other afterward.

Love is like that. It does the right thing toward the other. It says the hard thing when needed. In humility, it regards others as more significant.

When work teams commit to wholeheartedly loving God and one another, they can experience genuine family-style love, authentic harmony, and solid agreement for moving forward together.

CHAPTER TEN

Real Team

"It doesn't feel like we're a team, Lisa."

The words stung as I searched our staff member's face, looking for any sign of the personal rapport we'd built in his early years with us. It was gone. The ministry had grown significantly since then. Vision had expanded. Layers of supervision had been added.

"Can you help me understand what changed, what's wrong?" I asked.

He pondered his response. I could tell he didn't want to lash out in disrespect. Finally, he said, "I've had contributions I could've made that went untapped, input I could've given that no one asked for. There's a gap between leadership and others, a we/them mentality. I've felt underappreciated."

Suddenly things began to make sense—his distance, his clipped responses. I hadn't known what was causing that, and since his department didn't intersect with mine, I didn't cross lines to inquire.

I left the exit interview wishing we had asked him questions like that all along. Before it was too late.

I'd like to tell you this was before God brought the paradigm of relational community into our midst. But it wasn't. This was several years after. We should've known better. I should've known better.

But certain lessons are learned only in the glaring light of assumptions, offenses, and hard conversations. Biblical paradigms are from God, but they don't descend from heaven shaped, polished, and ready for use. No, they're forged in the day-in, day-out, learn-a-little, make-mistakes world of working and relating together.

So let's roll up our sleeves and look at practical ways we can be family together, loving our Father and relating more honestly and lovingly as brothers and sisters in Christ. And let's look at how to rebuild community when it begins to wane.

A Typical Community-Building Time

All our regularly scheduled meetings, which involve anywhere from two to twelve people, include a built-in portion of relational community. A two-hour meeting may start with thirty to forty-five minutes of "family time."

Here's a typical scenario.

At the beginning of a scheduled department meeting, one person is prepared with a topic for everyone to share about personally. We rotate leadership, since each staffer has a relationship with God, and the Spirit can lead him or her in deciding what to focus on. That can be a worship song, a verse or passage from Scripture, a question, an object lesson—anything to generate God-honoring conversation, help us get to know each other more deeply, and foster growth in Christlikeness.

For instance, the leader may place several small garden tools in the middle of the table—a hand spade, a dandelion weeder, pruning shears, and a watering can. He may read a passage about God being the master gardener and direct us to take a few minutes to ask the Lord which tool He's currently using in our lives. Then we each share about the tool God is using, the part of our life He's using it in, and the impact it's having.

Someone may choose the pruning shears and share how God is prompting them to cut back on a favorite activity so they'll have more time with family. Someone else may select the watering can and explain that they've been going through a spiritually dry time and know God is calling them to get away with Him for replenishment. Another person may pick the weeder to symbolize how God is putting His finger on a habit He wants to uproot. And then the leader invites each of us to pray for one other person.

Relational community provides an opportunity for everyone to share something personal in their life, so that people come to know each other as whole beings and not just by titles and responsibilities.

Sometimes there's a chance to give feedback or a word of encouragement. We may understand just a portion of what God is doing in our life, but others see God's work in us from a different angle and may be able to shed more light on it. In that way, they're helping us see God's perspective and become more Christlike.

As we grow closer to one another during this half hour or so of relational community, our connection as brothers and sisters sets the tone for the entire meeting. People feel safer with each other, we begin to understand strengths and weaknesses, and we're free to have vigorous discussions in which we share diverse opinions and reach well-rounded decisions. We seek to understand one another's perspectives, and we glean multifaceted wisdom from what God has revealed to each of us.

Maintaining Community during Disagreements

In one of our departments, a new staff member wasn't meeting performance standards. Her supervisor wanted to give her grace, and other team leaders agreed. As time wore on, though, the others could see that the individual didn't have the skills for the job. Still, her supervisor wanted to continue extending grace. But the staffer's performance kept falling short, and tension mounted in the department.

We were relatively new to relational community, and the department struggled through the difficulty. Tempers flared, and attempts to reach an agreement were met with resistance. Finally, we had an all-out, honest conversation. The supervisor admitted that she felt others were ganging up on her staffer, and she realized she was protecting that individual. But as the other leaders shared their perspectives, the supervisor came to understand that she wasn't viewing the performance shortfalls accurately. We agreed to part ways with the staff member.

Much headway was made because we pressed in to have that hard conversation. The supervisor became aware of her tendency to protect and hold on to a failing staffer. Department members committed to help the supervisor deal more quickly with poor performance. The team engaged in open communication during a difficult situation, grew to understand each other better, and became closer because of it.

Think about it—if we weren't committed to relational community and hadn't gotten to the real source of the supervisor's reluctance, we would've assumed she was just being stubborn or didn't value quality work or didn't care about how the poor performance was impacting everyone else. None of this was true, and left unaddressed, the problem—and the distance between team members—would've grown.

Pursuing relational community is invaluable in building up each other in Christ and forming closer relationships with one another. It helps us value and sharpen one another, so we can strive together to reach agreement and advance our mission. Our heavenly Father is pleased with our love for one another, and it gives Him glory.

Meetings That Include Relational Community

It's highly beneficial for every regularly scheduled meeting to include a time of cultivating relationships. In our ministry, this applies to leadership team meetings, department meetings, staff meetings, and board meetings. It also applies to supervisory relationships in which regularly scheduled, project-based meetings aren't necessary.

For example, we have a development assistant who, besides fulfilling her role on the development team, provides administrative support for me and our executive vice president. Since I don't meet with the entire development team, I miss the opportunity to connect more deeply with my assistant. To remedy this, we've created a special monthly meeting in which she and I and the executive vice president get together for an hour of relationship building.

You may wonder if a meeting like that is really necessary, since I interact with my assistant every day on both a personal and a project basis. But relational community goes beyond daily interactions. It provides a focused, uninterrupted time to foster authentic, Christ-centered relationships between supervisors and staff. In the rush to get things done, administrators can take other staffers for granted. But these staffers have equal value as people and equal value to the mission of the organization. An hour a month of relationship building is invaluable.

Basically, you'll want to ensure that every member of your staff is experiencing relational community at least once a month in a setting that's small enough for it to be safe, personal, and real.

As I've mentioned, at our headquarters, where twelve individuals work, we all meet once a week for an hour. We call it our Body of Christ Time, and the purpose is to connect with God and one another. But in a group that size, the level of sharing doesn't go as deep. Plus, there are four layers of hierarchy, which can be intimidating. So just because Sandy attends the weekly Body of Christ times doesn't mean she's covered. If she doesn't participate in department meetings, she should meet monthly with her supervisor for a time of relational community.

Comb through your staffers, segment them into departments, and see who's left. If there are support staffers who aren't included in department meetings, create a time for them to meet with their supervisor. If the support staffer is male and the supervisor is female, look for another person to join the group, someone who's a good fit based on project flow.

Signs of Absent or Eroding Community

The level of relational community throughout an organization can be inconsistent. There can be a pocket of healthy community in one department and a pocket of unhealthy community in another. If individuals aren't feeling connected to their supervisor or the community you're providing, they'll reach out for connection in other ways, not all of which are positive. God designed us for relationships, so people will find community one way or another.

For example, a few staffers who work closely together may find reasons to skip your corporate gatherings for worship and prayer. Or if they attend, they don't participate. Their demeanor begins to sour, and their interactions with the rest of the staff become stilted. They stop joining other staffers for lunch and start eating lunch with each other. This lack of involvement indicates an underlying problem worth investigating.

Or, in a small circle of staffers, there may be an unusually high level of rapport and personal relationships, which becomes exclusive. The intimacy of these staffers goes beyond a reasonable amount of interaction in the office setting. When you walk up to them, they change the topic of conversation. Sometimes you overhear negative remarks about their supervisor or the administrative team. Clearly, community is eroding.

At times, you may sense that some of your staff members aren't resonating with your leadership or vision. When you share new ventures at staff meetings, most of your staffers ask clarifying questions and join you in prayer, but a few of them remain aloof. Falling levels of cohesion and buy-in from certain groups of staffers indicate that something is amiss.

Reasons for Waning Relational Community

A common reason for lagging community is that it's not being provided by leadership consistently and effectively. Community doesn't come naturally for type A leaders, and it's easy to underestimate its importance in the stressful demands of the workplace. But if honoring God in an organizational setting is the sunlight that makes a plant grow, relational community is the water. Without water, the plant will wilt and die. Supervisors need to commit themselves to providing and participating in regular times of relational community with their staff.

Sometimes community declines because staff members have issues with authority in general, or they have specific issues with their supervisor. Left unaddressed, these problems lead to a growing distance between staffers and their leaders. We've found that when staffers withdraw from their supervisor, it's not only detrimental to their performance but also toxic to those around them.

The fallout from staffers being out of sorts with their leaders is that they sometimes don't express grievances appropriately. Instead of resolving the issue directly, they share their concerns laterally. Perhaps they're unsure of their own perspective and want a peer's viewpoint, but the result is that people hear negative comments about leadership, with no clear recourse. While these behaviors are common, they exacerbate the problem.

Community suffers when supervisors are either too busy to address relational problems or inclined to minimize their gravity. Most people don't like confrontation, and leaders are no different. We sometimes presume problems will work themselves out or that they'll stay contained to one or two individuals. But a problem with relational community almost always points to a deeper problem, and it needs to be dealt with.

Intervention When Community Is Lacking

When a staff member begins to pull back from community, their supervisor should speak to them about it with genuine concern, seeking to understand what's wrong. If a conflict or disagreement has arisen between the staffer and supervisor, the supervisor should work toward restoring the relationship, and resolving any performance issues, through times of honest conversation and community building with that individual.

Occasionally, a relational gap or conflict is significant enough that it's wise to seek assistance from a Christian mediator. This person will spend time with your leadership team and affected staff members to glean an understanding of the problem. He or she will suggest a biblical process for working together toward reconciliation. These meetings can be tenuous and uncomfortable, but they're helpful in airing grievances, seeking a shared understanding of what went wrong, expressing forgiveness, and committing to move forward together when possible.

If a staff member is performing well but won't participate in relational community, this is not in keeping with your organization's culture. When community is a core part of your culture, it becomes an essential criterion for employment. A nationally known CEO said he parts ways with staff members for two main reasons: poor performance and lack of participation in the organization's culture. The issue is that important. So, in our ministry, would we ever let go of a member of our staff who refuses to take part in relational community? Yes. We thoroughly convey its value to new staff members, share our expectations of their involvement, and explain that it's as essential to the health of the organization as fulfilling the requirements of their job description.

Welcoming Feedback in Relational Community

The essence of relational community is knowing each other as members of God's family, valuing each other's perspectives, and growing together in Christlikeness. One way to honor the perspective of every staff member is to ask them for input, feedback, and suggestions during regularly scheduled meetings.

Supervisors often make a blanket statement to new staffers about having an open door policy and wanting to hear any and all feedback. While these statements are made with sincerity, many individuals won't take their supervisor up on it. Call it respect, intimidation, or fear of reprisal—staffers often shy away from broaching difficult subjects with their supervisor. If they're not asked for feedback on a regular basis, they may assume it's not welcomed.

The responsibility for inviting feedback falls on the supervisor's shoulders, and feedback requests should be part of scheduled meetings, at least monthly. Staff members deserve a regular opportunity to answer questions such as:

How is your job going, workwise and relationally? If there are problems, what are your ideas about how we can address them together?

Do you have concerns, ideas, or feedback you'd like to share to help the organization in any area?

What would you change to make XYZ a better organization to work for?

Questions like these, whether asked verbally or in writing, will open up dialogue in order to nip problems in the bud and/or enhance aspects of the organization. Most staff members are highly invested in the organization's success and can provide valuable, objective perspective on both their own department and areas they're not involved in directly. Supervisors aren't obligated to implement every suggestion, but they are wise to consider them carefully.

Recently, I've begun meeting one-on-one with each of our twenty-five staffers, many of whom are at different facilities in nearby communities. The purpose is twofold: to foster relational community and to give individuals a chance to provide in-person feedback. These meetings have been mutually enjoyable, have made staff members feel honored and heard, and have been helpful to the overall function of our ministry.

We also conduct an annual survey to give members of our staff a more formal, comprehensive opportunity to share input or concerns in order to benefit the ministry. Organizations can create their own surveys or choose from one of the many effective online surveys.

Sharing Strengths and Weaknesses

One of our department heads was soon to join our leadership team as a vice president. In the months leading up to her role change, she participated in the relational community portion of the team's meetings. When it was her turn to lead, she asked each of us to share a story of how our God-given strength blessed another person. It was an encouraging time, and we all felt affirmed.

But then we began talking about the dark side of our strengths. I remembered a quote from a college professor: "Our greatest strength is also our greatest weakness." I shared with the group that as an exhorter, I am very open and loving toward others. Whether it's the woman in line behind me at Walmart or the man on the moon, I view most everyone as a soon-to-be friend. The downside to my porous heart toward others is that I'm also very open to others' opinions of me—or at least my perception of their opinions. The danger in this, of course, is that I can allow people's views to overshadow God's view of me.

Another member of our team shared that he tends to see people as a means to an end—a way to accomplish strategy. He has to remind himself that every individual is created by God and deserves to be valued and honored as a person, not just for the work they can do.

A wise leader said, "When you only share your strengths, you create competition. But when you also share your weaknesses, you create community." Now that my teammate and I know each other's weaknesses, I can help him make time to connect with staffers, and he can help me reorient to Jesus when I take a comment too personally.

Far from a mere Sunday school admonition, God's commandment to love one another has vast implications for the work setting. It leads to greater rapport, growth in Christlikeness, and ultimately—as everyone in the organization works in agreement toward shared goals—mission advancement.

CHAPTER ELEVEN

Advancement

"Ask Me for the building."

It was almost imperceptible, but impossible to ignore.

We were at our monthly meeting with intercessors, praying about high-level ministry issues. The one on the table was our need for a new building. Our ministry was expanding, and we'd outgrown our facility. We wanted to keep our existing building for headquarters, and purchase the building across the street for client services.

As we prayed, we told God how well the building would meet our needs and how we'd love to have it if it was His will. We tiptoed around asking Him for it, not wanting to be presumptuous.

But then one of our intercessors began reading Scriptures about praying in faith: "Ask, and it will be given to you" (Matt. 7:7), "Ask boldly, believingly" (James 1:6 MSG)," and a dozen similar verses.

We quietly contemplated those words.

That's when I heard it: "Ask Me for the building."

I wrestled internally. *Was that God's voice or my imagination? Does God want me to boldly ask Him for the building, because He wants us to have it? What if I pray that out loud, and everyone jumps on the bandwagon, and then we're denied the zoning variance we need to expand it? Talk about having egg on my face!*

Prior to prayer sessions like this one, I believed we were experiencing the productive pause in its fullness. Our teams were in unity with God and one another. We were honoring Him, loving each other, and learning to work well together.

But God had more for us.

He added to the mix discerning prayer—the third component of the paradigm of the productive pause.

I don't remember the day, the hour, or the specific issue God addressed. I just know that as we worshiped and read Scripture together, His perspective began to penetrate our minds. We gleaned new insights for our ministry. They were wise, fresh, divine. We prayed about them, implemented them, and the results were amazing.

But we didn't set out to implore God for help. Our initial focus was to worship Him and learn more of His infinite greatness. Remember the notebooks we filled with aspects of God's character? In our minds at that time, God was showing us the core of our culture—honoring Him. Starting our day with Him, worshiping Him, singing, reading Scripture, adoring Him. Simply yet profoundly, being with Him.

For me, it didn't have to become practical or productive. Exalting God was the endgame.

I'm sure God saw our sincerity. I believe He was pleased with our worship and glad we were replenished and revived. He reveled in our love for Him and our love and agreement with one another.

But He wanted more. He wanted to advance the ministry, and in His way. God's ways are higher and His thoughts are greater, and He wanted us to know them. He wanted to reveal them to us as we spent time in worship, in the Word, in discussion, and in prayer.

I've come to view the combination of worship and prayer as spiritual breathing. As we worship God, we breathe in the excellencies of His person. We connect with Him and His heart. As we pray, we breathe out the awesomeness of His ways and His wisdom, expressing what He's put in our hearts. It's a wondrous intermingling of Spirit and truth—our hearts drawing near to God's, and His truths permeating our minds.

I've quipped that when we pray without worshiping—without our hearts filled with an elevated sense of God—all the oxygen leaves the room. It can be suffocating. Prayer without worship is like one long exhale. Part of God's intention for worship is to fill us with His Spirit so we can pray God-sized prayers.

And so as we worshiped Him, God birthed prayers from our mouths.

Like when He said, "Ask Me for the building" during that prayer meeting. Let's pick up the story.

Oh brother, I thought as I sensed those words. In that moment, I had to decide which was worse: to step out in faith and look foolish or to ignore a prompting from God.

I tentatively began to pray.

"God, I'm sensing that You want us to ask You for the building. I think it may be Your will that we have it. So I'm stepping out onto what feels like really thin ice, and I'm asking You for the building. God, please give us 131 South 8th Street."

Dead silence.

But then the intercessor who'd read the Scriptures about faith joined in. Soon everyone got on board, and we all asked God for the building. We prayed that each room of it would be filled with people receiving love and services in Jesus' name.

We strode into the zoning meeting that afternoon, knowing God would grant us favor.

You can imagine my shock when the committee denied our variance. There could be no expansion on the property. The building became useless to us.

Kati and I walked away baffled, quietly trying to wrap our minds around what happened.

But God.

That same week, the building next to the one we wanted also came onto the market, their combined square footage easily meeting our needs. Before long we purchased both buildings, connected them with a throughway, and made plans to move in.

God had indeed met with us during that time of prayer, providing the authority of Scripture and the unction to pray in faith. He revealed His will that we would own the building, and He enacted it according to His plans. They weren't exactly what we'd expected, but His message to us was clear.

He essentially said, "Worship Me. Listen to Me. Agree with Me in prayer. I want to advance My ministry in My way, and I'll show you how to proceed."

That's the third principle of the productive pause:

Discerning God's wisdom brings advancement.

The Bible paints a vivid picture of the superiority of God's wisdom.

> "My thoughts are not your thoughts,
>   neither are your ways my ways,"
>   declares the Lord.
> "As the heavens are higher than the earth,
>   so are my ways higher than your ways
>   and my thoughts than your thoughts."
>
> —Isaiah 55:8–9 NIV

God draws a stark contrast between His thinking and typical human thinking. Simply put, they are nowhere near the same. His ways are so much higher, so much purer, and far superior.

Is your big hairy audacious vision starting to shrink? Mine is.

In the preceding verses, Isaiah exhorts, "Seek the Lord ... call upon him ... return to the Lord, that he may have compassion on [you]" (vv. 6–7). He describes a scenario in which we're functioning apart from God, according to our own thinking, and he urges us to cry out to Him.

God longs to be in relationship with us, and He also longs to show us His will and lead us in it.

"I will instruct you and teach you in the way you should go;
I will counsel you with my eye upon you."

—Psalm 32:8

"Call to me and I will answer you, and will tell you great and
hidden things that you have not known."

—Jeremiah 33:3

If any of you lacks wisdom, let him ask God, who gives
generously to all without reproach, and it will be given him.

—James 1:5

Clearly, God has supreme wisdom that He wants to share with us liberally.

Breaking It Down

Let's look at this final principle and break it down section by section.

**Because God is a Savior and we share His mission, we
earnestly discern His wisdom and obediently implement
His strategies. This results in advancement.**

1. "Because God is a Savior and we share His mission ..."

Every evangelical ministry and church and Christian business gets its chief motivation straight from the heart of God. He is a Savior. He doesn't want anyone to perish; He wants everyone to place their trust in Christ for salvation. God wants people to experience abundant life in Jesus, now and for all eternity. Ministries, churches, and Christian businesses go about this in a kaleidoscope of ways, but the core mission is the same—to help people know Jesus.

Who better than the Savior to know how to save? Who better than the Shepherd to know how to lead? Who better than Jesus to know how to disciple?

My point is this: reaching people is God's mission, and He knows how to do it. From the discipleship curriculum you use to your development department's philosophy, He has an opinion.

It's right. It's loving. It's smart. It's good.

And it's worth seeking and heeding.

2. "... we earnestly discern His wisdom and obediently implement His strategies"

The psalmist Asaph sought God's wisdom and experienced His guidance, all in the context of relationship. He wrote,

> I am continually with you;
> you hold my right hand.
> You guide me with your counsel,
> and afterward you will receive me to glory.
> Whom have I in heaven but you?
> And there is nothing on earth that I desire besides you.
> My flesh and my heart may fail,
> but God is the strength of my heart and my portion forever.
> —Psalm 73:23–26

Through the prophet Isaiah, God affirms His commitment to declare and accomplish His will.

> "As the rain and the snow come down from heaven
> and do not return there but water the earth,
> making it bring forth and sprout,
> giving seed to the sower and bread to the eater,

so shall my word be that goes out from my mouth;
it shall not return to me empty,
but it shall accomplish that which I purpose,
and shall succeed in the thing for which I sent it."

—Isaiah 55:10–11

Just as spring rains lead to harvest, God speaks His will from heaven and it happens on earth. It reminds me of the Creation account, in which God said, "Let there be light"—and there was!

A few years ago at our ministry, God said, "Let there be a new ministry model in the largest city where you have an outreach," and there was.

Here's the story.

God shifted us from serving abortion-vulnerable women at a single, full-orbed facility to serving multiple demographics of women through several streamlined locations.

This new approach wasn't even on our radar six months earlier when we met with our board to pray about ministry expansion. Steve, our vice president of strategic advancement, gave an overview of "dreaming out loud with God" and coached us to envision God's heart for the people we're serving and to see His enlarged vision for the future.

We worshiped together and began to pray. I wasn't sensing anything about the future, just God's desire that our hearts be one with His. So I thought, *I'll pray about that and get it out of the way, and then we can move on to the real prayer work—discerning God's long-term vision.*

I prayed that our hearts would beat according to God's, and that we'd remain in step with Him.

To my surprise, God was placing a similar line of thought in others' minds. One board member prayed we would run alongside God when He's running, and walk alongside Him when He's walking. Another prayed that in a fresh way, we'd surrender to the Lord our lives, the ministry, and our version of it. Others prayed in agreement.

Occasionally, Steve or I would interrupt the flow of the prayers to try to get things back on track—prayer for future ministry expansion. Steve prayed about a vision for helping other regions, and I prayed about helping life-affirming ministries internationally.

No one joined us. They continued praying about a greater oneness with God, a commitment to keep pace with Him, and an all-out surrender of the ministry.

Steve and I gave up after a few more attempts to sway God's heart toward ministry expansion, and began praying in line with the obvious theme.

Oftentimes in prayer, God will prompt a specific course of thought or direction, and it's best to persevere in that until it seems complete. God typically gives several people something to contribute to the concept He's building, and He usually doesn't jump around from topic to topic. You'd think Steve and I would've learned this already, but the captain in each of us can still have a hard time turning over the wheel of the ship.

After an hour of prayer, it seemed God had revealed His heart for this particular gathering, so we tabled the discernment of long-term vision for the next board meeting.

Amazingly, the theme of our prayer at the following meeting was more of the same—intimacy and surrender. And for the next four board meetings after that. Apparently, God wasn't ready to reveal anything more than His desire that we be in lockstep with Him. The predominant Scripture was John 12:24: "Unless a grain of wheat falls into the earth and dies, it remains alone; but if it dies, it bears much fruit."

Deepening our intimacy with God, keeping pace with Him, and surrendering to His will became our spiritual theme for that season. We'd taken notes in each of the prayer sessions and had a clear picture of God's heart, even though we didn't understand where He was leading us.

Fast-forward several months. Income wasn't keeping pace with expenses, and we had to make some tough decisions. I made a bold statement to my leadership team: "Well, mark my words. One thing we'll never do is close one of our locations." In my human thinking, I couldn't fathom God shortcutting ministry to people.

We held a retreat to glean God's perspective on the financial shortfall. Unbelievably, as we sought the Lord, He began speaking to us about the very thing I was unwilling to do—close a location. And our largest one, to boot! He used the verse "Unless a grain of wheat falls into the earth and dies …," pairing it with an allegory of a caterpillar entering a chrysalis and going through a metamorphosis to become a butterfly.

As we contemplated the allegory, its application to our ministry became clear. We pictured the closing of our largest location like the "death" of a caterpillar. It would be followed by a season of dormancy as we discerned the details of God's new model, which consisted of several smaller outreaches. They would be far more mobile, like a butterfly. The new model would also be more versatile and organic.

When we shared this with the board, everyone agreed that God had prepared us during those five months of prayer. We would take the difficult step of closing a location and accept this radical new model.

Three years later, instead of one large, stand-alone location, we established three smaller locations within the greater city limits— two of them housed in other ministries' buildings, and each reaching a particular demographic of women impacted by abortion.

God didn't shortcut His ministry to people. He creatively diversified it to reach the women who needed it most.

We were learning to discern God's wisdom, implement His strategies, and experience His advancement.

Discerning God's wisdom was Jesus' regular practice. He pressed in to perceive what His Father was doing, and He did it. He drew near to hear what His Father was saying, and He said it. This was possible because of their intimate relationship.

But let's pause here for an important distinction. Strategy never trumps relationship. Obtaining wisdom from God should never overshadow our relationship with Him. I can't imagine Jesus saying to His Father, "I want Your wisdom, but I don't want You." Jesus cherished and pursued His Father, and in the process He received His Father's wisdom and God's kingdom advanced.

At our ministry, and in our personal lives, we desire the same —first intimacy, then advancement.

Several years ago, I wanted to make a cabinet with my aging father. He was a master woodworker, having taught industrial arts for thirty-three years. Throughout my adult life, I bumped into guys who had Dad as an instructor and remarked about his skill and character. Many said he was their favorite teacher. I wanted to experience Dad this way.

So I became one of his students. He taught me to use a planer, a table saw, and many other tools. He'd guide a piece of wood through the planer, explaining as he went. Then I'd follow his example, with his hand over mine, helping me keep the board aligned. We worked side by side in our plaid flannel shirts, laughing, reminiscing, and getting covered in sawdust. Dad's expertise was obvious, but it was outshone by his love.

That's what drew me to make the cabinet—being with Dad, working together, receiving his love, loving him back. Yes, I have a great piece of furniture to show for it, crafted by my dad's wisdom. But the love we shared is the greatest takeaway from that experience.

In Colossians 2:2–3, Paul says, "being knit together in love, to reach all the riches of full assurance of understanding and the knowledge of God's mystery, which is Christ, in whom are hidden all the treasures of wisdom and knowledge."

Wisdom is hidden in Christ and is a by-product of being with Him.

Yes, we want to "get wisdom" (Prov. 4:5 NIV), but it comes as we say with Paul, "I want to know Christ" (Phil. 3:10 NIV). And it comes as we pray with Paul, "that the God of our Lord Jesus Christ, the Father of glory, may give you the Spirit of wisdom and of revelation in the knowledge of him" (Eph. 1:17).

Our highest calling is knowing our Father and Jesus (John 17:3). When we know Him, we'll hear His voice (John 10:16). When we hear His voice and His wisdom, we'll obey Him (John 15:9–10). And when we obey Him, His will is advanced in our organizations.

There's no better way; there's no greater privilege.

CHAPTER TWELVE

Spirit-Storming

The brainstorming droned on.

One hour, then two. Ideas swirled around the room like kites on steroids. It was a lofty topic, and sometimes the kites banged into each other, strings tangling. Voices rose. Disagreements erupted.

I'd offered to take notes and was busy clicking away on my laptop when the leader asked, "You haven't said much, Lisa. What do you think we should do?"

I was new to the group and no longer accustomed to this style of decision making. By this point, we'd been worshiping, praying, and discerning at our ministry for several years, and I was at a loss when it came to engaging in vital discussions apart from engaging with God.

"Um … I really don't know what to think about it. It's a serious issue, and … well, I'm sure God has an opinion on it. Maybe we could spend a little time worshiping and praying and see how He may lead our thinking and direct us through Scripture."

Does lead balloon come to mind?

No one knew what to say. Finally, someone countered, "Well, I think we all prayed before we came to this meeting." Another person added, "And we did open in prayer."

More awkward silence.

Then somebody ventured, "I think we should consider what Lisa suggested. I believe God would be honored if we stopped right now to worship and pray. And I bet we'll all be glad we did."

"I've got my guitar right here," someone else offered.

So we sang familiar worship choruses together, smack-dab in the middle of a high-level meeting. Then we prayed. Simple, straightforward prayers. Our awareness of God's presence increased, and His peace and perspective settled on us.

And that was the beginning of a group of seasoned ministry leaders learning to worship God and listen for His voice together when making important decisions. Two decades later, worship, prayer, and relational community are hallmarks of our gatherings.

Seeking God's Wisdom

So what's the difference between brainstorming and Spirit-storming? We coined the term "Spirit-storming" at our ministry as we noted the huge difference between tapping into our brains and tuning in to the mind of Christ.

Dictionary.com defines *brainstorming* as "a conference technique of solving specific problems, amassing information, stimulating creative thinking, developing new ideas, etc., by unrestrained and spontaneous participation in discussion."

We define *Spirit-storming* as "seeking God's wisdom and strategies by honoring Him through worship, talking to Him in prayer, reading Scriptures, freely offering up divergent thoughts and opinions in a Christ-honoring way, and watching God shape His direction."

Keith Yoder, a friend and mentor of our ministry—one of the two men who prayed for me when this whole journey began—taught us about discerning prayer in this way: "Picture that Christ is in the center of your group. He is Lord and He has wisdom for the issue you're praying about. As you acknowledge Him and His supremacy through worship and prayer, be sensitive to what He may be putting on your heart, and pray as He's prompting you. As you pray, imagine that you're laying your discernment before the Lord, and that it's just a piece of what will be discerned. Jesus will pick up portions of what the group has said, weave it together, and reveal His leading. You'll sense it as people begin to agree to a certain direction in prayer. There will be peace and confidence from the Lord to move forward."

The Underlying Concepts

Let's put this description into practice by unpacking the basic components of Spirit-storming. Over the years, as we grew in discerning prayer, these eight concepts became prominent.

1. God's Will

Our Father in heaven,
hallowed be your name.
Your kingdom come,
your will be done,
on earth as it is in heaven.

—Matthew 6:9–10

We're familiar with this prayer—it's the one Jesus shared with His disciples when they asked Him to teach them to pray.

In these verses, it's clear that God has a will. This is a heavenly version of what He wants to accomplish on earth. He may choose to reveal His specific will for us as we spend time with Him in worship, in the Word, and in prayer. When He does, we agree with Him by praying His will out loud. And His kingdom bursts into action on the earth, according to His will and His timing.

Sometimes I picture it like a well-thrown boomerang. Spirit-inspired prayer comes from God, enters our minds in agreement with Scripture, and—as we pray—returns to God in agreement with His will. Then He accomplishes His plan.

For example, at one of our biannual retreats, a board member prayed Matthew 6:9–10 for our ministry. As he prayed the part about God's kingdom coming "on earth as it is in heaven," I thought, *Well, since there are no abortions in heaven, clearly it would be God's will that there be no abortions on earth.*

In the ensuing weeks, I found myself praying that our region would be abortion free. Humanly speaking, an abortion-free region is hard to imagine. But God was emboldening my prayers. Soon other staffers were following suit. Before long, I spoke to the board member and told him how we'd been praying. I asked, "When you prayed that prayer, did you envision our region being abortion free?" He said, "Absolutely. I just didn't fill in the blanks."

The idea became a key component of our vision statement for many years:

Partnering with God for a salvation-full and an abortion-free region.

Spirit-led prayer can reveal God's will for all aspects of ministry. Nothing is too lofty or lowly for God to speak into.

2. Corporate Mind of Christ

Now we have received not the spirit of the world,
but the Spirit who is from God, that we might understand the
things freely given us by God....
We have the mind of Christ.

—1 Corinthians 2:12, 16

We, as believers in Jesus who are taught by the Spirit to understand spiritual truths, corporately have the mind of Christ. And just as iron sharpens iron, we hone each other, producing godliness in one another so that we function properly together. There's much we can learn from each other's perspectives and life experiences in Christ.

The same is true in discerning prayer. No single person has an exclusive ability to hear from God. We're all His sheep who hear His voice. Each of us can sense God's heart, and together our discernment makes evident the fullness of His wisdom. This means each person must be fully engaged, focused on the Lord, and willing to pray what they're sensing.

Years ago, Kati lost her husband after a sudden heart attack. Weeks later, it was time to discern the theme for our banquets. Neither of us could imagine praying about anything but her severe loss, so we spent the first forty-five minutes of our discernment time praying and grieving together.

Remarkably, as grief does when it's expressed, the sorrow lifted. God eased our emotions, and we were able to shift gears and discern His direction for the banquets. It was an astounding experience, and I asked Him in prayer, "What is this thing called grief?" Kati immediately envisioned a geode—a drab, rugged stone that when sliced open reveals beautiful crystals. It became for her a symbol of seeing God's beauty and goodness amid ugly pain.

God paired a question from me with an answer to Kati. Together we had the mind of Christ.

3. Agreement

[Jesus said,] "If two of you agree on earth about anything they ask, it will be done for them by my Father in heaven."

—Matthew 18:19

When believers discern God's will in keeping with His character and His Word, agreement in prayer is powerful. At our ministry, prayer times are often peppered with phrases like "I agree with Barry about ..." and "I agree with Deb that ..." This demonstrates that we're not only listening to what others are praying but also agreeing with it in our hearts.

It's okay to sometimes not agree or to discern a different part of the picture, but generally it's good to have a spirit of agreement during biblically-based prayer.

Recently, we leaned over a map of one of our outreach cities. A few staffers had visited nine areas of the city to explore possible satellite locations. They described each one to us, and we went to prayer. "Lord, where do you want us to locate?" As we discussed it with Him, we could tell which ones He was eliminating, and then which one He chose. When we prayed about that particular location, we sensed an added dimension of ministry. We sensed it would become a hub of intercession—for a renewed, citywide culture of life. As God painted the picture of His purposes for that location, excitement rose in our spirits. We agreed that this was the place God had chosen for us, and later we signed the lease.

4. Jesus in the Midst

[Jesus said,] "Where two or three are gathered together in My
name, I am there in the midst of them."

—Matthew 18:20 NKJV

This doesn't mean Jesus isn't with us when we pray by ourselves. It does mean there's a greater manifestation of God's presence and blessing when we join others. That's because our heavenly Father is a relational God, and there's a broader spiritual dimension when we're with our brothers and sisters in Christ.

Additionally, Jesus' emphasis on being in our midst is worth
noting. It goes back to Keith's description of Christ being in the
middle of the group. He is the centerpiece, and He's the one we're
talking to. It's important to keep this perspective as we pray, because it helps us focus on Him and stay attuned to the revelation
of His heart and direction.

At one staff meeting, we watched a video about a young woman
dealing with an unintended pregnancy. It was a creative and powerful portrayal of a scenario we'd dealt with hundreds of times. We
wanted our full staff to view it—especially those who weren't on
the front lines with clients each day.

Afterward, we entered into a time of prayer. As we talked to
Jesus about the video, He revealed how our hearts had grown cal-
loused toward the young women we serve. One by one, staffers in
client services asked God to remove the staleness and weariness
that had crept into their interactions with clients. We prayed that
God would give us His eyes and heart to see each woman as an
individual, created in His image and worthy of His love and ours.

There was an increased impact as we watched that video together, heard each other's hearts in prayer, and followed Jesus' di-

rection. Our hearts were cleansed as we drew near to Christ and He poured out fresh love for the people who come to us.

5. Spirit-Led Persistence

Pray without ceasing.

—1 Thessalonians 5:17

We typically view this verse as a command to maintain a spirit of prayer all day long, but it can also be interpreted, "Pray for something without stopping until you've covered it completely."

In other words, when God brings a topic to the forefront, it's important to remain focused on that until it seems finished. This will enable you to reach deeper levels of understanding and discernment.

For example, if you're praying about an annual event, and one person senses a celebratory theme, others should stay focused on that impression. As each person tunes in to what is currently being prayed and listens closely to the Spirit, they'll be able to add their own discernment to the mix. You may spend an hour praying about the theme, even though there are six other items on your list. But God may want to give you a deeper understanding of the theme first, and have the other aspects of the event follow suit. The important thing is to follow the Spirit in fully discerning one aspect before moving to the next.

As I shared in the previous chapter, when our board entered into a time of Spirit-storming for ministry expansion, God focused us on intimacy with Him, keeping pace with Him, and surrendering our version of ministry. We had to discipline ourselves to stay on topic with Him. As much as Steve and I tried to steer the prayers in a different direction, God won. And through those

Spirit-led prayers, He laid a foundation for a critical change of our ministry's model in the largest city we reach out to.

6. Piggyback Praying

> Agreeing wholeheartedly with each other ... and working together with one mind and purpose.
>
> —Philippians 2:2 NLT

We've already talked about the importance of agreement in prayer. This concept can be taken a step further as you and your teammates track closely with each other's prayers in order to "[work] together with one mind and purpose." In this way, you're piggybacking on one another's prayers, picking up where someone else left off. Sometimes it feels like you're finishing each other's sentences, because you're following along closely as they're praying, and your Spirit-led thoughts are headed in the same direction.

When you grow accustomed to praying this way, prayer becomes very conversational, as though you're all talking with the Lord together. Which of course you are! As we grew in prayer, we would track with each other, complete each other's thoughts, piggyback onto sentences ... and before long it would become so free and conversational that we'd ask each other, "Are we talking now, or are we still praying?" Then we'd laugh because we knew that prayer is simply talking with God. We were having a conversation with Jesus in our midst, discerning His will together.

When we prayed for a logo for our ministry, several of us were sensing the concept of new life for our clients. We pictured it in the form of fresh, green plant life and described it in prayer. As we kept building on each other's prayers, Scriptures about oaks of righteousness and leaves of healing came to mind. We looked them up and prayed them out loud. Through prayer and Scripture, God pieced together a beautiful logo of a sturdy, healthy tree with supple, green leaves, depicting His transforming power in our clients' lives. It served us well for decades.

7. Multifaceted Wisdom

His intent was that now, through the church,
the manifold wisdom of God should be made known.

—Ephesians 3:10 NIV

The Greek word for "manifold" is *polupoikilos,* which literally means "of differing colors." In the context of God's wisdom, it is "much varied, ultra diverse, with multitudinous expressions or facets" (HELPS Word-studies). Like an intricately cut diamond.

What a privilege to explore the facets of God's wisdom together through prayer and Scripture! As I've said already, every one of us has the potential to discern a portion of God's resplendent wisdom. Because God designed us as family and gave each of us a measure of His grace in our various giftings, His wisdom comes forth most fully when we all have a part in discerning it.

For the purpose of illustration, if ten people are gathered around a table in prayer, each person has the potential to discern a tenth of God's heart and wisdom on any particular topic. God may not parse out His wisdom in exactly this way, but the point is that as God's children, each of us is qualified to listen, to hear, and to share. This is how God's full counsel comes forth.

As someone senses something from God, it's his or her responsibility to step out in faith and pray it out loud—in essence, laying it before the Lord. The person may say, "I'm sensing that ..." or "I have the impression that ...," instead of praying, "This is what the Lord is saying: ..." In that way, we don't attribute it outright to God, and we also don't take ownership of what we've prayed. We release it to the Lord for His ultimate confirmation.

Similarly, if someone isn't sensing anything from God, it's wise for them not to contrive something just to make a contribution. In that case, the person should stay engaged and attuned to what others are praying, and pray in agreement when possible.

One year, as we discerned the T-shirt design for our Walk for Life event, God reminded us of a Scripture that was prominent in our ministry at the time. It was Isaiah 54:2, which says, "Enlarge the place of your tent, and let the curtains of your habitations be stretched out; do not hold back; lengthen your cords and strengthen your stakes." As we prayed, one person pictured a large tent, representing our ministry. Another person envisioned several tents, representing ministry expansion. Someone else saw the front of each tent opened wide, welcoming clients to our services. God weaved our discernment into a powerful T-shirt graphic of colorful tents paired with the reference for that verse.

8. Divine Synergism

Five of you will chase a hundred,
and a hundred of you will chase ten thousand.

—Leviticus 26:8 NIV

This verse lays out a powerful concept.

After several months of seeing the increased fruitfulness of corporate discernment, we started describing this phenomenon as "divine synergism." The effect of our combined prayers is exponentially greater than the sum effect of our individual prayers. Having prayed solo for years and experienced a certain degree of God's blessing, I found there was no comparison with the impact of group prayer.

God longs for and blesses our unity in prayer. As we pray together, faith increases, momentum builds, and God releases His wisdom and direction. There is much joy as God's will is revealed. Everyone has a part in the process, feels a sense of buy-in, and shares a commitment to obey God in seeing His will accomplished.

As we became schooled in prayer, God raised up a team of intercessors who met monthly with our leadership team to discern key issues. At one of our meetings, an intercessor began praying Jeremiah 18:4: "The vessel that he made of clay marred in the hand of the potter; so he made it again into another vessel, as it seemed good to the potter to make" (NKJV). The Scripture hit home, and we prayed at length that God would have the liberty to reshape the vessel of our ministry in any way He deemed appropriate. I sensed an image of another kind of vessel—a ship—making a slow, steady, ninety-degree turn to the left.

Over the next several months, I kept envisioning this ship making a significant turn. Our leadership team and board continued to talk and pray. We discussed the typical life cycle of ministry—vision, birth, growth, plateau, decline, and eventually death—if there's not a rebirth at the plateau stage.

We were in a plateau, and we knew it. Through more prayer, God initiated a rebirth of our ministry. We refocused our mission statement, streamlined services, adopted new core values, and put a new emphasis on discipling clients and reaching abortion-minded women.

All this began in prayer, when an intercessor faithfully shared a verse God laid on her heart. Thankfully, we had learned to listen to God's heart as we prayed and to watch what He was putting His finger on.

Our shift from brainstorming to Spirit-storming has served us well. Learning these concepts and putting them into practice has enabled us to reach beyond our human capacity and tap into the limitless wisdom of God. And the ministry advances accordingly.

CHAPTER THIRTEEN

Prayer at Work

"Maybe that's why I've been praying about Philadelphia for a year."

My mouth dropped open as our board chairman, Steve, spoke those words. (For years Steve served on our board; and later as a staff member.)

I was telling him about a new trend—opening pregnancy ministries in metropolitan areas. I'd just learned of it at a conference. Pregnancy centers are predominantly located in smaller cities, where churches and resources are plentiful. But in urban areas, where churches are sometimes strapped with the needs of their congregants and communities, pregnancy centers can be scarce. The thing is, there are far more abortions in metropolitan areas than in smaller cities and suburbs.

I recognized the problem but in no way thought we'd be part of the solution.

So Steve's words caught my attention. If God had been prompting him for a year to pray about Philly, surely there was something on His radar for us.

We decided to keep the concept under wraps and pray about

it. We were up to our elbows in planting another pregnancy center in our local community and didn't have the time or resources to think about a big-city outreach.

Months went by.

Finally, we were ready to announce the new location to our ten thousand supporters, through a newsletter to be mailed the day after our board meeting.

We started the board meeting with an extended time of worship and prayer. God led us to pray about stewarding our resources according to Acts 1:8—beginning in Jerusalem, then moving on to Judea, Samaria, and the uttermost parts of the earth. It seemed He was expanding the territory of our ministry.

Immediately after prayer, a board member said, "I'm wondering why we would open a sixth location in our two counties when Philadelphia, for example, has a much higher abortion rate."

Another member piped up. "I was just thinking the same thing!"

Steve and I looked at each other and grinned. I said, "I think we should tell them how we've been praying."

So we did. After a lengthy discussion and more prayer, God's will became evident and we were in agreement. We obediently decided to stop all progress on our new location. And those ten thousand newsletters hit the circular file.

Did you catch the progression of God's leadership in this scenario?

1. I learned of a new ministry model through others and at first didn't have the faith to pursue it.

2. God had already been stirring faith in the heart of our board chairman through prayer.

3. God led me to begin praying about this new concept with our board chairman.

4. During prayer at our board meeting, God revealed a broader calling on our ministry, and two board members suggested we consider reaching out to Philadelphia.

5. We traced God's handiwork, received faith through prayer, changed course, and began praying together about Philly.

That was over a decade ago, and I'll share another part of this story later. For now, let's look at some aspects of discerning prayer.

As this story demonstrates, as much as God wants us to know and obey His will, He's not bound to reveal it to us only during a prayer meeting or according to our timetable. While it's essential to set aside time for discerning prayer, it's equally vital to have your spiritual antennae up at all times.

That's what Jesus did. He spent a lot of time alone with His Father in prayer (Luke 5:16). He also focused on His Father in the moment—like when He healed a man on the Sabbath because, as He explained afterward to the irate Jewish leaders, He simply did what He saw His Father doing (John 5:1–19).

At our ministry, we regularly engage in discerning prayer, devoting significant time to it during leadership team meetings, board meetings, department meetings, and full-staff meetings. Additionally, whenever we need God's vision, wisdom, and direction, we set aside time to talk with Him.

But as I've said, God is not beholden to us. He's not a genie in a bottle who has to let us in on His will within our thirty to forty-five minutes of prayer. Sure, He draws near to us during that time and is pleased that we've drawn near to Him, but His wisdom and timing and overarching plan are beyond searching out. Romans 11:33 says, "Oh, how great are God's riches and wisdom and knowledge! How impossible it is for us to understand his decisions and his ways!" (NLT). Yes, He's a revealer of secrets—but again, in His way, in His timing, on His terms. He's a sovereign and wise God orchestrating untold events. We see through a glass darkly.

Lessons Learned

And so, while we've learned to spend time in discerning prayer, we've also learned to always keep our focus on God. We've learned to wait when things are unclear, to take note of God's silence, to pay attention to a lack of peace, to make sure everyone God wants at the table is there, and to keep on praying.

Wait for Clarity

Once, while discerning the theme for our banquets, we talked about inviting some clients to come and share their testimonies. While this is the bread and butter of any ministry banquet, it seemed to lack impact. Something was missing. So we decided to wait—both on God in prayer and to see if He'd speak another way.

Sure enough, God had more in mind. Over the next few weeks, we crossed paths with two volunteers who had compelling stories to tell. One was a hotliner who took a call from an abortion-minded client while she was literally on a roller coaster. The other had close friends who'd recently confided in her about their abortions. Both stories were a great fit for our banquets.

With these additional components, a theme came forth, and God put together a meaningful banquet program for our ministry partners. He did it through prayer, an initial sense of incompleteness, later conversations with others, and then agreement in prayer as He filled in the details.

Notice God's Silence

In another instance, developing a website was a priority in our strategic plan. Somehow it got squeezed out of every prayer time and leadership team meeting. We finally decided to schedule a separate meeting to tackle it in prayer and make some headway.

Unbelievably, as we prayed, God seemed to have nothing to say about the website. As much as we tried, we were getting no concrete direction and seemed to be praying in circles. As we acknowledged that to each other and before the Lord, He suddenly had plenty to say about upgrading the record keeping on our clients. So much so, that resolving our records issue became a priority over the next several weeks. We did eventually get clarity on a website, but at a much later point. We learned that God's silence speaks as loudly as His direction.

Heed a Lack of Peace

When God first placed the paradigm of the productive pause in our ministry, I had lots of invitations to share it with others. Before long, a group of leaders birthed a new ministry to share a similar paradigm, and I was asked to serve on its board. My board agreed, but with a level of hesitation because of the additional time commitment.

Month by month, I kept getting personal invitations to teach others about the paradigm, and I was also needed to help launch the new ministry. While my board recognized the importance of all this, they also carried responsibility for our own ministry. I could tell they were torn, and I felt torn too.

I distinctly remember the board meeting in which yet another invitation to speak about the paradigm was on the agenda. I felt a bit of dread as I pictured discussing it with my board. As we worshiped and prayed, God impressed on me the importance of placing all my activities under the authority and covering of the board—having their full blessing, not a reluctant one. He reminded me of the importance of agreement, unity, and peace.

In that interaction with God, the decision was clear. I would lay down my involvement with sharing the paradigm and trust God to lead into the future. As I shared this with the board, I could almost hear their sigh of relief. I was relieved too.

Several years later, one of our spiritual advisors said he sensed God wanted us to steward the expertise He'd entrusted to us. He shared that God wanted us to be servant leaders, not just in our own communities but also in the Acts 1:8 way I mentioned earlier—to people in Jerusalem, Judea, Samaria, and the ends of the earth. It was then that we all received the conviction from God that sharing the paradigm—along with other resources He was entrusting to us—was to be part of our ministry calling.

Ensure That Everyone's at the Table

As much as I'd shifted from discerning direction on my own to discerning with others, I still had a tendency to keep prayer groups too small. For example: For a season, Kati and I were the ones who decided how things should flow at headquarters, including whose office was located where.

At one point, we'd added a few staff and needed to reconfigure offices. Kati and I racked our brains with God and couldn't come up with a viable plan. *How could something so practical keep elud-*

ing us! I wondered. It was always easy to discern office locations. What changed?

As it turned out, it was more an issue of who was missing at the discernment table. We realized we hadn't included several staffers who carried significant responsibility and were skilled in administrative decisions like this. We invited them to join us for a prayer meeting, and—voila!—together we readily discerned the perfect office layout. The staffers were glad to participate in the process.

You'll want to use wisdom as you decide which people should be involved in any particular discernment issue, but don't assume it's the normal two or three. Always be open to include others who have a certain gifting or expertise that God may want to tap into as He reveals His will. You'll honor the individuals who join you, and you'll reap a fuller version of God's wisdom.

Abide in Prayer

Jesus abided with the Father 24/7, and we can too. When we care about a ministry and want God's best in it and through it, and abide with God continuously, He will speak His direction to us whenever and however He chooses. Two examples come to mind.

When God confirmed that we were to share our paradigm and resources with others, it required staffers who had writing expertise. At one point, we had a vacancy in the sexual integrity area of our ministry—an area where we were developing curriculum. One day, while I was walking down the hallway at work, it occurred to me that the husband of one of our staffers could be a great fit for that position. He taught high school students, had a passion for sexual purity and the sacredness of life, and had experience with curriculum writing.

I shared this idea with one of our vice presidents, and a smile broke across his face. He told me that another staff member had sensed the same thing. We did due diligence to vet and interview the candidate thoroughly, since his wife was already on staff, but he has been a great blessing to our ministry. And God initiated the whole thing by dropping the notion into several people's minds. Yes, much prayer followed those initial hunches, but God can speak outside of a prayer meeting. A burning bush comes to mind.

Another example: After viewing a video of a powerful client story at a staff meeting, it crossed my mind that the video could work well at our banquets. I pondered the thought for a while, prayed about it, and continued to feel positive about it. A few days later, I shared the idea with our vice president of development, and her eyes twinkled. She reached across her desk to retrieve a sticky note, on which another staffer had written, "Hey, what about using that client video at our banquets?" As we lifted our banquet program before the Lord in the ensuing weeks, He confirmed the video, and it became a poignant component of our banquets that year.

God loves to share His wisdom in various ways to various people, and He will do so to confirm His will.

Tracing God's Leadership

Acts 15 and 16 provide a striking account of how the apostles and elders practiced discernment. As you seek to grow in this third principle of the productive pause, an examination of these chapters would be a profitable, easy Bible study to undertake with your team.

When you read the chapters, looking for evidences of the productive pause, you'll see that the leaders

- considered and discussed matters together,
- based decisions on Scripture,
- exercised sound judgment,
- agreed on a course of action,
- discussed matters until they reached one accord,
- came into agreement with each other and with the Holy Spirit through prayer,
- were specifically led by the Spirit,
- experienced supernatural leading through a vision,
- made decisions together, and
- were influenced by a fellow believer who "prevailed upon [them]" (16:15).

Scripture encourages us to engage in all the practices listed here as we discern and follow God's will.

God used many of these practices to lead our ministry through a critical, mission-shaping period of discernment over several years.

Ten years into our ministry, a prominent leader in our movement urged me to network with other life-affirming ministries. She referenced John 17 and the role that unity among believers plays in helping unsaved people see Jesus' love in action. I understood the concept in theory, but it didn't seem at all feasible to me. It took everything I had to keep our own ministry afloat. How could I reach out to others without drowning?

But several years later, as we experienced the value of corporate worship and prayer, we naturally wanted to pass on to others what we had learned. We'd shared our new paradigm nationally and regionally through seminars, but we wanted to also live it out in our community.

We invited local leaders of life-affirming ministries to join us each month in prayer. Gradually—because of the unifying power of worshiping and praying together—the walls between us began to fall. We prayed that we would release our solo mindset and stop working independently. We prayed that even though our ministries had different names, the unifying name over all of them would be Jesus. We prayed that we would get to know each other as individuals, that we would learn about each other's ministries, and that we'd make sure there were no overlaps or gaps in our services to clients. And over time, that's what happened.

As I mentioned earlier in this chapter, God used one of our spiritual advisors to point out a servant-leader calling on our ministry, a calling to partner with other ministries and steward the wisdom and expertise He had entrusted to us. While it was encouraging to hear this commendation, it carried a heightened sense of responsibility to serve others, beyond our clients. We spent many months in prayer and discussion to discern how to restructure our ministry accordingly.

But it was unmistakable that God was speaking to us through others, through His Word, and through our prayer and discussion. He was urging us to

- discard our silo mentality,
- foster unity with other ministries,
- cultivate relationships with other ministry leaders,
- steward the resources He had entrusted to us, and
- discern together how to join hands for the sake of His kingdom.

It could be summarized in the phrase "Seeking intentional partnerships to steward resources and advance the kingdom."

This phrase formed the foundation for the story I began telling at the beginning of this chapter—how God turned our hearts toward the people of Philadelphia.

When we first learned of the need for additional pregnancy ministries in urban communities, our initial thought was, "If Philadelphia needs more pregnancy centers, we should plant a few there." That would seem logical, right? There's an apparent void, and the obvious answer is to fill it.

But God's ways are higher than ours, and His logic is too. As we prayed, God helped us understand that the local leaders in Philadelphia had the best read on what their city needed. While we may have had objective input to offer, it would be shared only in the context of authentic relationships.

So our heart and strategy turned to relationship building. We would reach out to pregnancy ministry leaders in Philadelphia, with a genuine desire to know them as individuals and hear about their vision and mission and ministry issues.

Transformation happens at the speed of relationship, and we knew this would take several years. And it did. But God is Lord of Time, and we were at peace knowing we were in agreement with His heart and will. So we took our time in developing relationships with our brothers and sisters in Philadelphia. And God has begun to do what only He can do.

Watch the domino effect of God's blessing when ministries begin working together:

1. As we developed relationships with the leaders of one of the pregnancy ministries in Philly, we learned they wanted to add ultrasound scans to their services. This is a hefty

undertaking, and a key component is an expensive ultrasound machine.

2. Meanwhile, God prompted a local Christian leader to raise the funds needed to purchase a brand-new ultrasound machine for us.

3. His gift freed us to donate our used—but still very viable—ultrasound machine to our friends in Philadelphia. They were thrilled, although they couldn't put it to immediate use because they lacked the facility for it. But God had a plan.

4. One of our supporters offered to make a sizable contribution so we could purchase a mobile unit to provide ultrasounds for our clients. We explained that we didn't have the client load for it, but our friends in Philly did. So we referred him to the Philadelphia ministry.

5. He contacted them and made the contribution, which set the wheels in motion for them to purchase a demo model mobile unit at a reasonable price.

6. Months later, the mobile unit drove onto their property and became the perfect vehicle to house our donated ultrasound machine.

7. Their staff is now trained to provide ultrasounds, and women throughout Philadelphia—from neighborhoods to college campuses—are seeing and bonding with their preborn baby, rejecting abortion and choosing life.

All because God wants us to be one with our brothers and sisters in Christ, and He enables us to discern His heart as we seek Him together.

Discerning prayer will help you know God's heart, vision, principles, and strategies for your organization. You may have a general understanding of His will for your church, ministry, or business, but just as God led His church leaders very specifically in Acts 15 and 16—and just as He's led us—He wants to lead you.

CHAPTER FOURTEEN

How Strong Is Your Knot?

Ron and I were perplexed.

After we purchased a used boat so we could explore more of the Thousand Islands, we began noticing plaques in people's boathouses, saying things like,

The second-best day of your life is when you buy a boat; the best day is when you sell it.

A boat is a hole in the water that you throw money into.

Surely, it couldn't be that bad.

Oh, how naive we were.

Blissful rides on sparkling blue water would be interrupted by horrible scraping thuds as our propeller struck hidden shoals.

When Ron started the boat after launching it one spring, white smoke plumed from the engine compartment.

Once, the throttle got stuck as we were going full speed ahead in a boat-strewn river—thrilling or terrifying, depending on how you're wired.

The most horrifying occasion followed the white smoke incident.

The boat was freshly back from the mechanic, and as we loaded up family members one evening, Ron assured me all was well. But partway around a large island, I noticed he was glancing at the gauges as he gave commentary on the eighteenth-century mansions gliding by.

I slid beside him and whispered, "Is everything okay?"

"Well," he whispered back, "the oil pressure is running high. But it's better than running low."

That meant nothing to me, so I decided to help Ron monitor the gauge. When the needle climbed farther, I asked, "How serious is it when it's in the red?"

"It's not good, but at least it's not beyond there."

Ron began pausing longer than usual to look at houses, resting the engine. But when he resumed speed, the needle soared beyond the red zone. My blood pressure did the same.

Both of us acted as if everything was fine. But dusk was falling, and we still had twenty minutes to go.

Our guests were happily clueless and became enthralled at the sight of a freighter up ahead. Its stern rose above us as we caught up to it. When we overtook the behemoth, Ron slowed down so everyone could admire it. And to give our engine another break.

We passed the ship, and before long our dock was in sight. I was never so happy to see our peaceful little cottage beckoning us home.

But just as Ron made his final turn, the engine died. No power. No electricity. Nothing. Ron poked his head under the dash to see if any wires were disconnected, but he couldn't find the problem.

Then his brother shouted, "Hey, Ron, that freighter's heading this way!"

Ron shot up and started firing orders at everyone. "Grab the oars! Start paddling!" Suddenly we were in a full-scale emergency. Our tiny boat was no match for the freighter, and that monster could never turn in time to avoid us. Dead in the water took on new meaning.

We found only one oar. It was useless against the current, which was sending us directly into the freighter's path.

"Yell for help!" Ron hollered as he opened the engine compartment.

We all started waving our arms and crying "H-e-l-l-l-p!" to anyone who would listen. An elderly woman on the shore heard us. Cupping her hands to her mouth, she yelled back, "I'll call the coast guard!"

A lot of good that would do. By the time they showed up, we'd be flotsam. Or jetsam—I never really understood the difference.

A couple boats passed us, apparently deciding they weren't up for the challenge.

There weren't many boats on the river, but finally a large cabin cruiser pulled up beside us. The captain had assessed our situation and acted swiftly. He threw us a rope tied to the back of his boat and shouted, "Tie this to the ring on your bow!"

Ron leaned halfway over the front of our boat, secured the rope, and the captain quickly pulled us toward the riverbank.

As we caught our breath, he asked, "Where are you headed?"

"Just a half dozen docks upriver—the little brown cottage after the blue one," Ron answered.

"Here's what we need to do," the captain explained as our boats jostled in the wakes. "I need more space between us to maneuver safely past your dock, so get one of your ropes, untie mine, tie yours to the front of your boat, and join the two ropes." He added emphatically, "And use a good square knot."

We scrambled for our longest rope. Ron crawled over the bow again, untied the captain's rope, tossed it to us, and started tying our rope to our boat. My brother-in-law grabbed the two rope ends. He asked me if I knew how to tie a square knot. I didn't. So he intertwined the ropes as best he could, pulled them tight, and held up the tangled mass.

"What do you think?"

"Looks good to me," I said.

He flung the extended rope overboard, and it hit the water with a splash.

To my horror, in order to stay clear of shallow water and rocks along the shoreline, the captain began circling back to the center of the seaway—right into the path of the freighter.

It suddenly became vital for that knot to hold.

I searched the river's surface for the limp rope. I watched it slowly lift off the water. There in the middle was my brother-in-law's knot, looking like a boy scout's first attempt.

The rope grew taut. I stared at the knot, willing it to hold.

Our boat began to move forward. The knot held.

The captain led us in front of the freighter and then back toward our cottage. He measured his approach and slowed nearly to a stop as our boat moved within reach of our dock.

We grabbed the dock, untied the ropes, and threw him his line. As he throttled away, we yelled thanks and held out a twenty-dollar bill.

He gave a neighborly wave, as if to say, "It's all in a day's boating experience. You can pay me back when you see someone else stranded on the river."

And we have. Once you've been rescued, you never drive past a boater in trouble.

So the question is, how strong is your knot? How strong is your personal connection with your heavenly Father? How strong is your corporate connection with the Founder of your organization? How well are your team members growing in Christ and in working together? Is your mission advancing according to God's heart and wisdom? Do productive pauses with God and one another characterize the ebb and flow of your workdays?

Tying It All Together

Let's look at the three principles of the productive pause as we unpack this story and draw parallels to our work lives.

Honoring Lordship Brings Alignment

When the captain of the cabin cruiser pulled up beside us and began barking orders, it was obvious who was in charge of this rescue operation. He was clearly experienced and had already thought through his plan.

Ron was still the leader on our boat, but now he was carrying out the captain's instructions.

As we instinctively honored the captain, an alignment took place. We became attached to his boat. Where he went, we followed. Even when the path he chose seemed dangerous—as he circled back in front of the freighter—we trusted that he knew what he was doing.

God is hands down the Captain of our organizations. He is the Birther, the CEO, the very present and active Leader. He's a seasoned, take-charge kind of God. As we honor Him, we become connected to Him. We abide with Him. And through that oneness, our hearts, minds, and actions align with His.

A beautiful symmetry of movement follows.

If you had watched our boat follow the captain's, you would've seen two vessels traveling as one. On the same path, at the same speed, toward the same destination.

And that's the fruit of honoring lordship. Togetherness. Oneness. Singleness of heart and mission. Alignment.

Cultivating Relationships Brings Agreement

Did we know the captain when he pulled up? The quick answer is no. But the pondered answer is yes. We knew he cared. We witnessed his skill in pulling beside us in choppy water. We could tell he understood our crisis. We felt his authority as he gave instructions. All that in the first thirty seconds. Yes, you could say we knew him. Enough to trust and obey.

And we knew Ron. Before the captain showed up, Ron was our navigator, our tour guide, our mechanic. When the crisis hit, we looked to him and did everything he said. We paddled. We yelled for help.

And we knew each other. We were family. We were in this together—initially on a joyride around the island, and then on an escape mission to avoid the freighter. We caught and tied ropes. We looked to each other and reassured each other.

We weren't quite a well-oiled machine, but we loved one another and cared about each other's safety. We were in agreement about getting off the river in one piece. And afterward, as we sat around the campfire reflecting on the experience, we laughed. At the way Ron bolted upright when my brother-in-law mentioned the freighter. At the slow circle our boat made as we paddled with all our might. At the sight of Ron stretching over the bow and nearly falling overboard. At the frantic way my brother-in-law's hands moved as he tied that knot.

Most of all, we felt closer to God, who ultimately was the one who rescued us. We also felt closer to each other, having shared such a crazy experience.

When we purpose to know our great and powerful God together in the work setting, our corporate relationship with Him begins to grow, and eventually it flourishes. We enjoy Him. Talk with Him. Obey Him. Love Him.

When we intentionally connect with our coworkers as brothers and sisters in Christ, and strengths shine and weaknesses bleed through and opinions are given and blind spots are identified and mirrors are held up and truth is lovingly spoken—well, that's when deep agreement can be reached.

And a ragtag group of children can walk hand in hand with their Papa and each other, confidently following wherever He leads them—much as a band of travel-worn disciples, aligned and in agreement, followed their Lord to Gethsemane and eventually to the uttermost parts of the world.

Discerning God's Wisdom Brings Advancement

In our boating incident, the captain had the most wisdom. He'd no doubt sat behind the wheel of his vessel for years, reading navigation charts, avoiding shoals, negotiating wind and wakes, docking in unfavorable conditions.

And I'm sure we weren't the first desperate crew he helped.

His wisdom became gospel to us. We obeyed every word to the best of our ability. And it worked. We advanced with Him. We made it safely home.

God holds out to us His presence, His heart, and His wisdom. That's His constant posture. At the ready. Toward us in a relationship of love.

He is filled with joy when we reciprocate. When we turn toward Him. When we love Him back.

He loves to hear us talk to Him about our mission, and He loves to share His wisdom so our mission can advance.

He's the Captain we're tethered to—giving instructions, ensuring we're attached, leading the way. Whether the seas are calm or stormy, He guides us on the best course for success.

So the productive pause yields alignment, agreement, and advancement. But at its core, it's about relationships. It's about loving God and others.

As you implement this new paradigm, start there. Go for the gold of honoring relationships with God and one another. Revel in newfound intimacy with Abba. Marvel at His greatness. Settle into His goodness. And deepen bonds with coworkers. Celebrate strengths. Press into weaknesses. Help each other be melded to Christ and molded into Christlikeness.

And in the course of all that, feel your corporate spine straighten with God's strength. Notice coworkers laying down tug-of-war ropes and joining together on the same side. Hear the beautiful rhythm as you all move in harmony with God's direction and strategy—not in military formation but in a family dance. Sometimes resting. Sometimes running. Always abiding. Keeping pace with God.

Worship creatively. Love God and each other passionately. Seek and obey God's wisdom wholeheartedly. Follow His lead meeting by meeting—any Spirit-led combination of these will bring honor to His name and joy to your hearts.

Alignment. Agreement. Advancement. You will experience these awesome, kingdom-building outcomes.

But the pursuit and the prize will always be Jesus Christ Himself.

An Open Letter to an Exhausted Leader

I see you. I know you. I've been you and still am at times.

I feel your angst. I see your clenched jaw. Your darting eyes. The harried glance at your watch.

I see the load you're carrying, the responsibility, the expectations. I see how it crushes the life out of you—although you work hard to hold yourself together. The smile remains, the show must go on. You don't mean for it to be that way, but on some level it is.

I bump into you at a leader's conference, and your sentences are filled with the activities that crowd your calendar. You mention how people can depend on busy people like you because busy people get things done.

And I wonder about the body count at your workplace, in your home. Who's drowning in the wake of your frenzy?

And how's your own heart doing? Who do you unload it to? Do you?

When do you breathe? When do you rest? When do you savor a sunset or watch a toad till he moves? When do you play? Do you?

I imagine you've skimmed through this book to get to the end—just like I'm still tempted to do—because there's no time for savoring and changing. I imagine that Mr. Time has his grip on you, making you run faster and accomplish more than you ever thought possible.

What if it's actually not possible? What if it's not profitable? What if it's not even Abba's will?

What if His will looked a whole lot simpler, a whole lot more sane? What if it looked like a whole new landscape at your organization? Or was greater than anything you ever dreamed? What if He wanted to be Lord—literally. What if He wanted to take over? What if He asked for the reins? What would you do?

What if He wanted to transform your ministry by transforming you? What if He wanted you to take a sabbatical—for a day, a week, a month, or three? What if He wanted you all to Himself? Would you go?

What if He wanted to pour His love into you like never before? What if He assured you that He's already pleased with you—apart from your accomplishments? What if He wanted to expand the ways you worship Him and connect with Him and learn from Him? What if there was more that He wanted to give you? More ways to be together? Would you go there?

If you took a sabbatical, how would your team survive? Are they connected to the Vine—together, as a group? Can they discern God's wisdom apart from you?

How about their relationships with each other? Are they honest? Are they real?

Do they express opinions and give input? Do you ask for it? Are you open to it? Are you growing together in Christlikeness? Are you holding up mirrors for each other?

What if all this took more time than you think there is? What if it feels like one more mountain to climb, and you're not up to it? What if the surge of hope you've felt as you read this book leaves you disenchanted in another month, when life continues at NAS-CAR speed?

Here's my word to you.

Pause.

Pause and listen. Listen long. Listen hard. Listen well. Listen for His voice.

He's your Shepherd. He designed you to hear His voice. He knows the first thing He wants you to do.

Maybe you felt His nudging as you read this book. Maybe it was about honoring Him at work. Maybe you played through a scenario in your head: I could ask Jack and Amanda to join me. I think they'd be okay with it. Maybe a worship song came to mind, a song you'd listen to together. Or maybe one will.

Guaranteed, God will speak to your heart about this paradigm of His. He knows it in its totality, and He knows you in yours. He knows how He'll lead you into it. And He knows what the very first step will be, and whether it will be a baby step or a long jump.

So relax. Breathe. Enjoy these moments of anticipation.

Surely, the Lord is in this place—this place where you are right now.

Surely, He is with you.

Surely, He is mighty to save, mighty to change you and your organization.

Surely, He is.

Surely, He will.

So pause. Listen. Receive His prompting. And take the first step.

You can be an unexhausted leader whose greatest goal and reward is God Himself. You can be replenished by streams of living water from His Spirit and His Word. You can be inspired by His greatness. You can lead your teams in seeking and loving and being with and hearing from and obeying God.

You can, because He wants this for you. His invitation stands.

"Come to Me, all who are weary and burdened, and I will give
you rest. Put My yoke upon your shoulders—
it might appear heavy at first, but it is perfectly fitted to your
curves. Learn from Me, for I am gentle and humble of heart.
When you are yoked to Me, your weary souls will find rest. For
My yoke is easy, and My burden is light."
—Matthew 11:28–30 Voice

This is the pathway to becoming an unexhausted leader. This is the essence of the productive pause—Jesus Christ and you and your team yoked together in intimate, restful, replenishing advancement.

Postscript & Dedication

Several months after this book was written and on a publishing path, my husband Ron was diagnosed with terminal brain cancer. I spent the next 13 months at home with him as we journeyed with Jesus through the rigors of radiation and chemotherapy. Jesus was ever present and wise. The body of Christ was extremely loving. The cancer treatment was grueling. The suffering was horrific. All of it, a mixture of tragedy and triumph, with Ron's final triumph being his entry into heaven on September 23, 2019.

As you saw through the personal stories in this book, Ron was full of life and adventure. He was also my best friend, confidant, and ministry supporter through our 32 years of marriage. He witnessed my personal transformation as the events of this book unfolded, as well as the remarkable revolution within the ministry. He was so glad I was able to capture it in book form to share with others.

And so it's in honor of Ron that I kept the book in its original time frame and present-day language, before his diagnosis.

Ron, I dedicate this book to you. To whom you were on this earth as my husband, leader, and friend. And to whom you are in heaven as the Father's son and Jesus' friend, reveling together in the fullest version of the productive pause.

About the Author

Lisa Hosler is anchored in the Word — God's written Word and the Living Word, Jesus. With a bachelor's from Lancaster Bible College and master's from Millersville University, God called her in 1985 to lead Align Life Ministries.

Lisa's leadership is characterized by followership. As you'll read in this book, she looks for, listens to, and responds to God's generous direction.

I joined the staff in 1994 and have seen Lisa's active alignment to God and what it yields. The productive pause is the culture of the ministry. I've repeatedly experienced the peace-filled power that God brings through it, whether in times of great fruitfulness or intense difficulty.

Along with being a strong leader, Lisa is a Jesus friend to me. There's always been an ease and enjoyment between us. Yet when God brought the added dimension of intentional honesty, He gave me the gift of Lisa caring more about me being like Jesus than whether I bristled at her frank feedback. Jesus consistently challenges, strengthens, and loves me through her. I'm deeply grateful.

Lisa's whole-hearted passion is to know Jesus, and He has given her His heart for others to know Him. She lives an unwavering consistency of belief, words, and actions. Her Jesus-centered, God-yielded integrity makes Lisa a most trustworthy vessel for Him to speak the paradigm of the productive pause through. May you be challenged and transformed by the truth within these pages.

— **Kati Swisher**
Executive Vice President, Align Life Ministries

Contact Information

Read more from Lisa by visiting her blog at www.lisahosler.com.

Contact Lisa with questions, comments, or speaking opportunities by emailing her at lisa@lisahosler.com.

Learn more about Align Life Ministries at www.AlignLifeMinistries.org.

Made in the USA
Monee, IL
26 January 2022

89814811R00115